Danny Pecorelli
MANAGING DIRECTOR

My favourite place of sanctuary has always been by a hotplate in one of the hotels, watching as the hours of effort and years of learning get distilled into the dish constructed on the plate. Each of the dishes will reflect the different personalities of the chefs, his or her style, passions, culinary history and current thought process. This book is the opportunity for you to take home and try the recipes and personalities of a very eclectic and talented collection of British chefs.

A number of things do however bind together these chefs: a passion for seasonal, fresh local produce and a drive to support the best local and regional suppliers. We are after all a collection of English Country Houses with British chefs at the helm. So much of the food we get in hotels and restaurants can suffer the same ills as some of the pre-packed homogenised supermarket meals readily on offer, produced in industrial quantities full of no-one knows what, presented on a plate to the unsuspecting public as 'home made food'. Not only is this not proper food - it does nothing to support and promote the local food heroes who abound in this country. We have tried to highlight a number of our 'local food heroes' in this book, to show that the chef has to be an equal partner to his suppliers. To produce exceptional food you need exceptional ingredients. The more we all try to stop food being commoditised and ensure the food chain returns to a local level, the better for all of us.

Food and wine have always gone together and to complete the meal experience our sommeliers have chosen wines to complement each dish. The right wine can truly enhance a dish, which is why we now have every wine on our lists available by the glass, so that each course can be matched by the perfect wine.

I do hope that the vibrancy of our kitchens can be translated into your kitchens at home. These dishes are not difficult to make, they just require a little time, effort, passion for life, a large glass of wine and an appreciative audience.

Enjoy

CONTENTS

EXCLUSIVE HOTELS

Andy Mackenzie
HEAD CHEF

I started work as a Chef at the age of 16. My first job was at The Springs in Wallingford, where I worked on a three-year apprenticeship with day release to attend college.

I moved on to the Four Seasons in London, called The Inn at the Park, in Park Lane, where I worked as Third Commis Chef, moving up to First Commis Chef and then Demi Chef de Partie.

I began working at Lainston House in 1986, taking over the pastry section as the Pastry Chef was away for six months. I had originally planned to stay within Winchester and at Lainston House for only a year, but I found I was able to express my cooking at Lainston, making dishes and putting together recipes I had always dreamed of. So although I had been planning to move to France and build a life over there, I changed my plans and decided to stay. I progressed to Sous Chef, and then three years ago became the Head Chef.

I became a chef because I feel so passionate about food, I love cooking and the different dishes I can produce. Being made Head Chef has given me a chance to express my passion for food, I have had so much inspiration from Gary Rhodes, his simple good British foods, and have been lucky enough to work with such exceptional chefs as Mark Manaw, Paul Beaucoup and Raymond Blanc.

I met my wife Sarah working at Lainston House, whilst she was working on the breakfast shift, and we have three children, Aimée, James and Jack. Having begun cooking from an early age with my Mum, the passion just grew from watching her and learning all that she knew. I love to cook for my family and spend time with them when I am not working.

Please enjoy my recipes and cook with passion.

Lainston House Hotel

MENU

LAINSTON HOUSE HOTEL

CHICKEN LIVER AND FOIE GRAS PARFAIT
*with truffle butter, danebury jelly,
and warm toasted brioche*

POACHED PORTLAND LOBSTER SALAD
mango salsa, lemon mayonnaise

GRILLED 'BOSWORTH ASH' GOATS CHEESE
caramelised figs, red wine syrup (v)

CANON OF HAMPSHIRE LAMB
*mediterranean vegetables, gratin potatoes
and garden mint fritters*

WILD SEA BASS
*tomato pesto, courgette spaghetti,
watercress purée, saffron tuile*

STOCKBRIDGE ORGANIC WILD
MUSHROOM FRICASSÉE (V)

VANILLA CRÈME BRÛLÉE
with honey ice cream and sesame tuile

PEACH AND CHABLIS JELLY
with elderflower sorbet

GOOSEBERRY AND CUSTARD SOUFFLÉ

CHICKEN LIVER AND FOIE GRAS PARFAIT WITH TRUFFLE BUTTER, DANEBURY JELLY, AND WARM TOASTED BRIOCHE *(serves 4)*

INGREDIENTS

PARFAIT
360g chicken livers
150g foie gras
100ml ruby port
100ml Marsala
60ml brandy
60g banana shallots
2 cloves garlic
1 level tbs dried thyme
1 bay leaf
650g butter (*at room temperature*)
6 eggs (*at room temperature*)
1 level tbs salt
3g ground white pepper
$^1/_2$ level tsp pink salt
(*to keep the chicken livers pink, can be bought in any good delicatessen*)
1 small loaf tin lined with cling film

DANEBURY JELLY
70g sugar
120ml Danebury sparkling wine, or a dessert wine
1 leaf bronze leaf gelatine

TRUFFLE BUTTER
120g unsalted butter
10ml truffle oil

METHOD OF PARFAIT
Pre-heat the oven to 100°C/220°F/Gas Mark ¼. Peel the shallots and the garlic, chop, and sweat slowly in a pan with a little oil for 8 minutes. Add the alcohols, the thyme and the bay leaf, and boil together until reduced to one third. Strain and set aside. Blend the eggs and the alcohol reduction together in a liquidizer or food processor, and add the softened butter little by little, incorporating it well each time before you add more. Blend the chicken livers and the foie gras into the egg mixture whole, add the salt, pepper and pink salt. Blend further. Pass the mixture through a fine sieve, and place in a small terrine lined with cling film. Place the terrine in a bain marie in the oven and cook until the centre of the terrine reaches 70°C (you will need a thermometer for this which can be bought in any good kitchen appliance shop). Once core temperature has been met, remove the terrine from the bain marie (being careful not to scald yourself), and leave to cool at room temperature for 30 minutes before placing in the refrigerator. Leave to chill for 24 hours before turning out of the terrine.

METHOD OF DANEBURY JELLY
Bring the Danebury wine and the sugar to the boil. Soak the leaf of gelatine in a little water until soft, then squeeze out the water and melt in the hot wine syrup. Leave the jelly to set. When set, whisk until frothy and place in a piping bag, ready to pipe and serve.

METHOD OF TRUFFLE BUTTER
Blend the unsalted butter and truffle oil together until soft. This is the *chemise* (shirt) for the parfait. Using a palette knife spread a thin layer of truffle butter evenly around the exposed sides of the parfait. Refrigerate until the butter has set. Turn the parfait onto its side and repeat the process on the remaining side. Refrigerate until ready to serve.

TO SERVE
Slice the parfait with a hot knife and place on a chilled plate. Pipe jelly around the edges of the parfait, and serve with warm toasted brioche.

TO DRINK...

**Tokaji-Pinot Gris,
Colmar, France 2003**
A demi-sec, floral
white wine

POACHED PORTLAND LOBSTER SALAD, MANGO SALSA, LEMON MAYONNAISE (serves 2)

INGREDIENTS

LOBSTER
1 lobster (*750g in weight*), ideally caught off Weymouth shores and bought alive to ensure freshness

MANGO SALSA
200g diced mango
200g tomatoes (*peeled, deseeded and diced*)
20g finely chopped red onion
20ml balsamic vinegar
60ml olive oil
1 tbs finely chopped coriander
Zest of 1 lemon
Salt and cracked black pepper to taste

LEMON MAYONNAISE
100g mayonnaise
(*at home I prefer to use Hellmans*)
Zest and juice of one lemon
Salt and pepper to taste

GARNISH
1 punnet sakura cress or some young salad leaves

METHOD OF LOBSTER
To kill the lobster take a large sharp knife and cut the head in half lengthways by inserting the point of the knife halfway down the natural centre line, bringing it down with force. Plunge the lobster into boiling salted water and cook for 9 minutes. Remove lobster and chill in iced water. Once chilled, crack the claws and joints and remove the meat in one piece. Split the body from head to tail. Remove the tail meat from each half and remove the track (bloodline), with a small knife; wash the meat if necessary.

METHOD OF MANGO SALSA
Mix all ingredients together. Leave to marinate for 2 hours.

METHOD OF LEMON MAYONNAISE
Grate the lemon zest finely, and mix into the mayonnaise with the strained lemon juice. Adjust seasoning to taste.

TO SERVE
Dress the plate with lemon mayonnaise or serve on the side if preferred. Serve the lobster with a generous helping of mango salsa and garnish with a little cress or some small salad leaves.

LAINSTON HOUSE HOTEL

TO DRINK...

Chablis Premier Cru, Fourchaume, La Chablisienne 2001
A lightly oaked white wine with a floral aroma

GRILLED 'BOSWORTH ASH' GOATS CHEESE, CARAMELISED FIGS, RED WINE SYRUP (V) *(serves 4)*

INGREDIENTS

4 large slices of goats cheese

STOCK SYRUP
120ml water
70g sugar
1 slice of orange
1 slice of lemon
$\frac{1}{4}$ of a stick of cinnamon
1 bayleaf

CARAMELISED FIGS
6 figs halved lengthways
(3 *halves per portion*)
20ml stock syrup

CHUNKY TOMATO DRESSING
100 ml stock syrup
100g tinned chopped
tomatoes in juice
100g drained tinned
chopped tomatoes
10ml aged balsamic vinegar
2 tsp finely chopped parsley
2 tsp finely chopped chives
1 tsp finely chopped shallots

RED WINE SYRUP
100ml Madeira
100ml port
100ml red wine
30g brown sugar

CHEF'S TIP

We use plenty of chervil for
a light anise flavour.

METHOD OF STOCK SYRUP
Boil all the ingredients together for 2 minutes, take off the heat and leave to infuse for 20 minutes. Strain through a sieve and chill, discarding all the ingredients in the sieve.

METHOD OF CARAMELISED FIGS
Leave the figs to marinate in the stock syrup for 30 minutes, face down. Slowly caramelise the figs until golden brown in a medium-hot frying pan, being careful not to burn them. Put to one side.

METHOD OF CHUNKY TOMATO DRESSING
Blitz the tinned chopped tomatoes in juice, together with the stock syrup, in a food processor. Add the balsamic vinegar, herbs and shallots, blitz again. Pass this through a fine sieve and mix together with the drained chopped tomatoes, season with salt and pepper and refrigerate.

METHOD OF RED WINE SYRUP
Place all the ingredients together in a thick-bottomed pan. Reduce until a syrup consistency. Keep warm.

TO COMPLETE AND SERVE
To serve, drizzle red wine syrup onto a serving plate, followed by the chunky tomato dressing. On a tray slowly grill the caramelised figs to re-heat and place them on the plate. Place one generous slice of Bosworth Ash goats cheese per portion on top of the figs. Lightly season with cracked black pepper and a drizzle of olive oil. Return to the grill and leave until the cheese is soft and lightly coloured. Place one portion of figs and cheese onto the plate and garnish with the herb of your choice.

TO DRINK...

Morgento, Campania, Italy 2003
A dry and crisp white wine

CANON OF HAMPSHIRE LAMB, MEDITERRANEAN VEGETABLES, GRATIN POTATOES AND GARDEN MINT FRITTERS *(serves 4)*

INGREDIENTS

2 loins of lamb prepared by your butcher from 1 short saddle off the bone, with each loin cut into 2 pieces.

GRATIN POTATOES
1500g Maris Piper potatoes *(washed, peeled and thinly sliced 4mm)*
450ml double cream
450ml milk *(preferably full fat)*
2 sprigs rosemary
4 cloves garlic, crushed
6 sprigs thyme
Salt and pepper to desired taste

GLAZE FOR GRATIN POTATOES
80ml double cream, 1 egg yolk
30g finely grated Parmesan

MEDITERRANEAN VEGETABLES
1 whole aubergine
1 red pepper , 1 yellow pepper
1 onion, peeled and finely sliced
4 plum tomatoes, sliced lengthways
1 green courgette, sliced across into ovals
1 yellow courgette, sliced across into ovals
Olive oil for cooking

GARDEN MINT FRITTERS
A handful of mint
Fritter batter:
100g cornflour, 100g self-raising flour
$\frac{1}{2}$ tsp bicarbonate of soda
10ml white wine vinegar
70ml sparkling water
Pinch of salt and pepper

200ml vegetable oil for cooking

METHOD OF GRATIN POTATOES

Pre-heat the oven to 190°C/375°F, Gas No 5. Bring all the ingredients except the potatoes slowly to the boil. Once bubbling, remove the herbs, add the sliced potatoes and bring back to the boil, stirring continuously. Line an ovenproof dish with greaseproof paper, pour this mixture into it, and bake for 30-45 minutes or until the potatoes are cooked and golden brown.

METHOD OF MEDITERRANEAN VEGETABLES

Preheat the oven to 140°C/275°F/Gas Mark 1. Bake the aubergine for 1½ hours until soft. Slowly caramelise the sliced onions and peppers in a little oil in a thick-bottomed pan. Slice the baked aubergine in half longways and scoop the cooked flesh into a bowl. Mix with the caramelised vegetables and place on top of the cooked gratin potatoes. Arrange alternate slices of tomato and courgette on top of the vegetable mixture. Return to the oven for a further 7 minutes.

METHOD OF GLAZE FOR GRATIN POTATOES

Mix all the ingredients together. Spread the glaze over the Mediterranean vegetables on top of the potato gratin, and place under a hot grill until golden brown.

METHOD OF GARDEN MINT FRITTERS

Mix together all the dry ingredients for the batter, and slowly whisk in the water and vinegar, to form a coating consistency. Heat some vegetable oil in a deep pan. Strip the mint leaves from the stalks, coat each leaf in batter and fry carefully in the hot oil until crisp, turning once. Drain on kitchen paper; season with salt.

METHOD OF LAMB

Pre-heat the oven to 200°C/400°F/Gas Mark 6. Cook the four pieces of lamb, fat side down, in a medium to hot frying pan until golden (about 4 minutes). Turn the lamb over and cook for one further minute to ensure it is completely sealed. Roast for 5-6 minutes to reach medium to rare cooking. Slice the lamb and serve as shown in the photograph, with a rich gravy of your choice (for ideas, see the sauces included in the recipe for Sausages and Mashed Potato *(page 110)* or the recipe for Sautéed Lambs Kidneys *(page 64)*.

TO DRINK...

Brunello di Montalcino, Ferrero, Tuscany 1999, Italy
A soft tannin, fruity red wine

WILD SEA BASS, TOMATO PESTO, COURGETTE SPAGHETTI, WATERCRESS PURÉE, SAFFRON TUILE *(serves 4)*

INGREDIENTS

SEA BASS
4 x 200g fillets wild sea bass
(scaled and pin boned)
Ask your fishmonger to
prepare this for you

TOMATO PESTO
3 red plum tomatoes
(skinned, deseeded and diced)
1 small shallot
$^1/_2$ clove garlic
5 basil leaves
1 tbsp tomato purée
150ml extra virgin olive oil
5g white wine vinegar
20g sugar
6g salt

WATERCRESS PURÉE
8 x 25g packets watercress
5g salt

COURGETTE SPAGHETTI
4 green courgettes

SAFFRON TUILE
1 medium-sized red
skinned potato
1 pinch saffron

METHOD OF TOMATO PESTO
Place the tomato, garlic, shallots, and basil in a food processor and slowly mix together. Add the tomato purée and mix well. Slowly add the olive oil and vinegar until the mixture forms a sauce. Season to taste with salt and sugar.

METHOD OF WATERCRESS PURÉE
Remove the stalks from the watercress and place the leaves into boiling water for 3-4 minutes. Remove and refresh the watercress in a bowl of iced water. Drain and dry well. Place in a food processor and blitz until smooth. Add a little salt to taste.

METHOD OF COURGETTE SPAGHETTI
Take 4 courgettes, de-seed and cut into thin slices longways and cut again to make thin strips. Blanch these in boiling water for 3-4 minutes. Remove from the heat and add to a bowl of iced water (to refresh). Dry, and leave to one side.

METHOD OF SAFFRON TUILE
Peel and chop the potato and boil with the saffron. Drain and dry well. Place in a food processor and blitz until smooth. Add salt to taste. Take the potato paste and press thinly into shapes. Place on greaseproof paper and dry in a very low oven until crisp.

METHOD OF SEA BASS
Sear the fillets of sea bass in a hot non-stick pan with a little oil for 3-4 minutes each side.

TO SERVE
Assemble the dish by placing the fish on top of the reheated courgettes tossed in a little butter and seasoning. Drizzle the pesto around the dish and place a spoonful of watercress purée on top. Garnish with the crispy tuile.

LAINSTON HOUSE HOTEL

TO DRINK...

Pinot Blanc, Willi Opitz, Spätlese, Austria 2002
Creamy and buttery with a long finish

21

STOCKBRIDGE ORGANIC WILD MUSHROOM FRICASSÉE (V) *(serves 4)*

INGREDIENTS

VEGETABLE STOCK
120g leeks
60g carrots
60g celery
1g coriander seeds
5g garlic
4g thyme
5g curly parsley
45ml white wine
125g plum tomatoes
1 litre water
5g salt
1 tbs olive oil

PASTA
330g 00 grade flour
3 eggs
1 yolk

PERSILLADE
25g parsley
25g banana shallots
8g garlic

MUSHROOM FRICASSÉE
600g assorted organic
wild mushrooms
3 plum tomatoes
Persillade
Vegetable stock
Vegetable oil
100g unsalted butter

Shavings of parmesan
to garnish

METHOD OF VEGETABLE STOCK

Peel all the vegetables and cut into 1cm dice. Heat the olive oil in a thick-bottomed pan. Add the leeks and carrots and cook very slowly for one hour, until caramelised. Add the celery and cook for 30 minutes more. Crush the coriander seeds using a pestle and mortar, and add to the vegetables with the garlic, thyme, parsley and wine, and boil for 30 seconds. Add the chopped plum tomatoes and continue to cook slowly for a further 30 minutes. Add the water and salt, and simmer for a further 45 minutes, skimming frequently. Strain through a fine sieve.

METHOD OF PASTA

Blend the flour, eggs and extra yolk together in a food processor until a dough is formed. Leave to rest in a refrigerator for 1 hour before use. Roll on a pasta machine down to number three on the dial. Once rolled, pass through the linguini attachment and blanch for approximately 20 seconds in boiling salted oiled water and refresh in iced water. You can then cook them in boiling water as you need them, once you have finished the mushroom fricassée.

METHOD OF PERSILLADE

Peel and finely chop the shallots and the garlic. Pick over and wash the parsley. Chop it very finely and mix with the shallots and garlic.

METHOD OF MUSHROOM FRICASSÉE

First plunge the tomatoes into a pan of boiling water for 10 seconds. Remove and place in a bowl of iced water (to refresh). Once cool, skin the tomatoes. Cut into 4 wedges and scoop out and discard the seeds. Pat dry with kitchen paper and cut into small dice. Place a little vegetable oil in a hot frying pan and sauté the wild mushrooms until soft. Add 300ml vegetable stock. Add the persillade and bring to the boil. Now add the butter while stirring continuously, and at the very end add the diced tomatoes.

TO SERVE

Twist the linguini with a fork and place in the centre of a warm bowl. Spoon the mushroom fricassée around the pasta and finish with shavings of parmesan or a hard cheese of your choice.

LAINSTON HOUSE HOTEL

TO DRINK...

**Leabrook Estate,
Pinot Noir, Adelaide
Hills, Australia 2002**
A rich red wine with
a raspberry bouquet
and a long finish

23

VANILLA CRÈME BRÛLÉE WITH HONEY ICE CREAM AND SESAME TUILE (*serves* 4)

INGREDIENTS

BRÛLÉE

125g egg yolks
(*requiring probably 7 or 8 eggs if they
are large, but you really will need
to weigh them to do this recipe justice*)
75g sugar
125ml milk
370ml double cream
1 vanilla pod (*cut in half
and seeds scraped out*)
4 tbs demerara sugar

HONEY ICE CREAM

250ml milk
250ml whipping cream
12 egg yolks
250g sugar
100g glucose syrup
25g honey or to taste

SESAME TUILE

50g butter
75g sugar
50g flour
50g egg white
1 tsp sesame seeds

CHEF'S TIP

Try using other flavours by
replacing the honey with
ingredients such as vanilla,
strawberry syrup/purée
or even Pernod.

METHOD OF BRÛLÉE

Preheat the oven to 100°C/215°F/Gas Mark ¼. Put all the ingredients into a bowl and mix well together. Divide the mixture between 4 ramekins. Bake in the oven for about 45 minutes or until set with a very slight wobble. Take out and leave to cool. Before serving sprinkle the top of the brûlées lightly with brown sugar and caramelise either with a blow torch or under the grill.

METHOD OF HONEY ICE CREAM

Mix the yolks, sugar and glucose together. Place the milk and cream in a saucepan and bring to the boil, then pour onto the eggs while whisking fast. Return the mixture to the stove and cook stirring continuously until the mixture thickens slightly. When ready, place the pan in a bowl of iced water to halt the cooking process. Stir in the honey and strain the mixture. Place into an ice cream maker and churn until frozen.

METHOD OF SESAME TUILE

Cream together the butter and sugar until soft. Add the flour and the egg whites a little at a time to form a smooth paste. Spread the tuile mix thinly onto a sheet of greaseproof paper or non-stick baking paper and sprinkle with sesame seeds. Bake in the oven at 150°C/300°F/Gas Mark 2 until lightly brown. Take out and cut into triangles whilst still warm, then leave to harden.

TO SERVE

Place a scoop of ice cream on top of each crème brûlée and then place the tuile on top of the ice cream.

LAINSTON HOUSE HOTEL

TO DRINK...

De Bortoli, Noble One, Botrytis Semillon 2000, Australia
Apricot and honey rich, sweet dessert wine with a long finish

PEACH AND CHABLIS JELLY, WITH ELDERFLOWER SORBET *(serves 4)*

INGREDIENTS

JELLY
400ml Chablis wine
50ml water
50g sugar
5 leaves bronze leaf gelatine
(soaked in cold water until soft)
1 white peach
(poached with the skin removed)

ELDERFLOWER SORBET
250ml water
100g sugar
70g glucose syrup
100ml elderflower cordial
$^1/_2$ lemon, zest and juice

CHEF'S TIP

This recipe will work with almost any other fruit that isn't too acidic, for example, kiwi or pineapple.

METHOD OF JELLY
Boil the water and sugar together to make a syrup and mix in the soft, drained gelatine, which should dissolve almost immediately. Add the Chablis wine. Purée two thirds of the peach with a hand blender and add to the jelly mixture. Strain the jelly and pour into your chosen moulds. Dice the remainder of the peach and divide between the moulds. Place in a refrigerator and leave for 3 hours or until the jelly has set.

METHOD OF ELDERFLOWER SORBET
Boil together the water, sugar, glucose and lemon zest and juice to form a light syrup. Add the elderflower cordial, and strain the mixture. When cold, churn in an ice cream machine* until frozen.

TO SERVE
Turn jelly out of mould by dipping the mould very quickly into a bowl of hot water and place onto a cold plate. Place a scoop of sorbet next to the jelly and garnish with a sprig of mint.

* If you don't own an ice-cream machine; you can leave the mixture to freeze in a stainless steel tray and scrape the sides into the middle regularly with a table fork during the latter stages of freezing. This will give you an end result similar to sorbet, and its name is granita.

LAINSTON HOUSE HOTEL

TO DRINK...

**Moscato d'Asti,
Bel-Sit,
Piedmont 2004**
A fruity and slightly
sparkling sweet
wine with a low
alcohol content

GOOSEBERRY AND CUSTARD SOUFFLÉ *(serves* 4)

INGREDIENTS

COMPÔTE AND SOUFFLÉ

300g gooseberries

50g sugar

5 egg whites

45g sugar

CUSTARD

125ml milk

125ml double cream

1 vanilla pod

3 yolks

75g sugar

25g cornflour

CHEF'S TIP

To avoid overcooking your custard once it has reached the right consistency, place the base of the pan in a large bowl of iced water, and stir constantly.

METHOD OF CUSTARD

Bring the milk, cream and vanilla pod to the boil in a saucepan. Mix the egg yolks, sugar and cornflour together in a separate pan. Pour the boiling liquid onto the mixture, stirring well. Return to the heat and stir constantly until the mixture has thickened.

METHOD OF GOOSEBERRY COMPÔTE

Cut the gooseberries in half, place in a saucepan with 50g sugar, and simmer until soft. Strain off and reserve the juice.

METHOD OF SOUFFLÉ

Place 1 tablespoon of the compôte and 1 tablespoon of custard into 4 medium sized buttered and sugared ramekins. Whisk the egg whites with the sugar until firm peaks form, and then gently fold in 2 tablespoonfuls of the gooseberry juice. Place the mixture into a piping bag and pipe into the ramekins into a high dome shape. Bake in the oven at 200°C/400°F/Gas Mark 6 for 8-9 minutes.

TO SERVE

This dish works well as it is or alternatively you can serve it with a scoop of vanilla ice cream.

LAINSTON HOUSE HOTEL

TO DRINK...

**Danebury Sparkling
Wine 2000, England**
Fresh appley flavour
with a long perlage

29

June Cheeses – June

IN ORDER SERVED ON PLATE - 12'O'CLOCK, M

11'O'CLOCK – STRONGEST

July Cheese.

(1) Luddesdown – Welsh, fresh, zesty goats
soft melting texture

(2) Lon Pevre – Southern France, Citrus flavour G

_____ ____ ___ _____ which is a secon

____ _____, _____ strong/fruity taste. (semi-

(5) Bleu des Basques – From South west France
Mild and sweet, creamy blue veined sh

Lune TAB GRABBER

Karl Edmunds
HEAD CHEF

I have worked in some of the most beautiful places and fantastic restaurants. I worked at Le Meridien Piccadilly and also at the Martinez hotel in Cannes, in the south of France, where my favourite restaurant to date, the Palme d'Or restaurant is located. It is amazing, and would be where I would choose to dine if given the chance to go to any restaurant in the world.

I was brought up in a miners' village in Kent, and I became interested in cooking at a young age. I used to cook cakes with my Gran and then on going to school I was inspired by my cooking teacher to learn much more. I cooked my first dish at the age of 14: it was a huge family Christmas meal, turkey and all the trimmings. After leaving school I became more and more passionate about food, learning from the catering teachers and fellow students at Catering college.

I have been lucky to have worked with some exceptional chefs and I admire anyone in the industry for their commitment to do the job professionally and to succeed to the highest level. It is such a buzz to perform to your greatest achievements, I am proud to say that by the age of 23 I was already a Head Chef.

I have been working at Pennyhill Park for 16 years, growing and showing my passions in the kitchen; within the first year of being at Pennyhill I had earned 3 AA Rosettes. Something I continue to be proud of.

Like many chefs, your kitchen is your life and spare time is hard to come by. I met my wife at Pennyhill and we now have three children; my wife continues to work at Pennyhill also.

If I am not cooking I like to spend time with my family, playing football and ice-skating. My family and my food are my life.

Pennyhill Park Hotel

MENU

PENNYHILL PARK HOTEL

CHICKEN LIVER TRIFLE
balsamic jelly, red onion marmalade

DUBLIN BAY PRAWN, GLAZED PORK BELLY
with english asparagus

COLSTEN BASSET STILTON SALAD
with walnuts and pear

TADLEY FOREST VENISON
with parsnip, blackberries and a juniper jus

'TOAD-IN-THE-HOLE'
with pork and apple sausages

LIGHTLY POACHED TURBOT
with crumbled biscuit of hazelnut and olive, fennel foam

RHUBARB AND GINGER CRUMBLE
with devonshire clotted cream

ELDERFLOWER JELLY
with fresh english berries and pressed raspberries

BAKED VANILLA RICE PUDDING
with victoria plum compôte

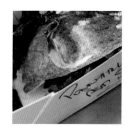

CHICKEN LIVER TRIFLE WITH BALSAMIC JELLY, RED ONION MARMALADE (*serves* 4)

INGREDIENTS

PARFAIT
200g fresh chicken livers
200g melted butter
2 free range eggs
Brandy to taste
75ml double cream
Salt, pepper, pink salt

REDUCTION
100ml port
100ml Madeira
1 shallot, chopped
2 sprigs thyme
2 cloves garlic, crushed

BALSAMIC JELLY
250ml balsamic vinegar
100ml chicken stock
1 tsp honey, 4 leaves gelatine

TOMATO COMPÔTE
8 plum tomatoes
2 tbs tomato purée, Olive oil
2 cloves garlic, finely chopped
2 shallots, finely chopped
8-10 basil leaves

RED ONION MARMALADE
6 sliced red onions, 20ml olive oil
100ml crème de cassis
50ml red wine vinegar

GARNISH
4 cherry tomatoes
Olive oil, 4 sprigs of basil

You will need
4 piping bags, if possible

METHOD OF REDUCTION
Place all the ingredients in a small saucepan and boil to reduce to a syrupy consistency. Strain.

METHOD OF CHICKEN LIVER PARFAIT
Preheat the oven to 125°C/240°F/Gas Mark ½. Line a small terrine mould with cling film, making sure that the edges of the cling film overlap the top of the terrine mould. With the ingredients at room temperature, blend the livers with the reduction and then the eggs. Finally, slowly add the butter. Strain into the terrine, place in a bain-marie (or water bath) and cook in the oven for 45 minutes. Cool, then refrigerate. Cream the parfait with the brandy, cream and seasonings. Place in a piping bag and leave at room temperature.

METHOD OF BALSAMIC JELLY
Soften the gelatine in cold water. Warm the balsamic, chicken stock and honey in a saucepan. Squeeze water from the gelatine, add to the warm mixture and stir to dissolve. When cold, strain and refrigerate. Turn out, chop finely, place in a piping bag and return to the fridge.

METHOD OF TOMATO COMPÔTE
Remove the eye from each tomato. Blanch in boiling water for 10 seconds, plunge into iced water and remove the skin. Halve, discard the seeds and roughly chop the flesh. Sweat the shallots and garlic in olive oil until tender. Add the tomato flesh and tomato purée. Cook to a compôte, season to taste and cool. Shred the basil into julienne strips and add to the compôte. Place in a piping bag.

METHOD OF RED ONION MARMALADE
Sweat the onions in a little oil until soft. Add the vinegar and cassis, cooking slowly until 'jammy'. When cool, chop finely and place in a piping bag.

METHOD OF SEMI-DRIED TOMATO GARNISH
Score the bottom of cherry tomatoes, leaving the stalk on. Blanch in boiling water for 4-5 seconds, plunge into iced water and remove the skin, leaving the stalk intact. Place on a baking tray, season with salt, pepper and olive oil, and cook at the lowest temperature until semi dried, about 45 minutes.

TO SERVE
Assemble the ingredients in layers in a champagne glass. Top with a semi-dried tomato, a sprig of basil and a teaspoon of onion marmalade. Serve with toasted brioche or rustic bread.

TO DRINK...

**Riesling,
Egon Müller 2004,
Germany**
Complex aromas
of lime, apple and
exotic fruits, long
off-dry finish

37

DUBLIN BAY PRAWN, GLAZED PORK BELLY WITH ENGLISH ASPARAGUS (*serves* 4)

INGREDIENTS

GLAZED PORK
4 x 30g pieces of pork belly
5 carrots
2 onions
3 sticks celery
2 leeks
Water to cover
4 tsp honey

PRAWN PARCELS
12 langoustines (*Dublin Bay Prawns*),
shelled and with
intestines removed
6 spring roll paste sheets
(*from a supermarket*)
1 egg, beaten
6 long cocktail sticks

VELOUTÉ
200g onions/shallots
1 tbs olive oil
400g asparagus trimmings
1 litre chicken stock
400ml double cream
200ml dry white wine

GARNISH
40g frisée lettuce
40g lollo lettuce
8 asparagus tips, blanched

METHOD OF PORK BELLY
Roughly chop the carrots, onions, celery and leeks, and place in a baking tray with the pork belly. Cover with water and cook in a very low oven at 85°C/185°F/Gas Mark ¼ for 10-12 hours. Remove the pork and place on a tray or plate. Leave to chill overnight in the fridge with a flat weight on top (eg. another tray/plate the same size, with weights standing on it). Next day, cut into 2.5cm squares and leave in the fridge.

METHOD OF LANGOUSTINES
Skewer 2 langoustine tails onto a cocktail stick and wrap in a spring roll sheet, sealing it carefully with the beaten egg. Continue until all the langoustine tails are wrapped - 6 sticks each with 2 langoustines. Refrigerate until needed.

METHOD OF VELOUTÉ
Slice the onions and cook in the oil until soft, without allowing them to brown. Add the white wine and the chicken stock, and boil to reduce until the pan is almost dry. Add the cream and boil again, to reduce by half. Then pass though a sieve. Bring back to the boil, add the asparagus trimmings and cook until tender. Liquidise in a blender until smooth, then sieve, and set aside in the fridge.

TO COMPLETE AND SERVE
Pan fry the squares of pork belly and cover with honey in the pan to produce a glaze. Season the lettuce leaves with salt and pepper and olive oil and place on the plate, sit the pork belly on the centre of the lettuce leaves. Reheat the velouté, blanch the asparagus tips, and fry the langoustine parcels for 1 minute at 180°C/350°F/Gas Mark 2. Once cooked, remove the cocktail sticks and cut the tubes in half. Arrange on the plate and lean the asparagus tips against the langoustines. Drizzle with the velouté sauce and serve immediately.

PENNYHILL PARK HOTEL

TO DRINK...

**Sauvignon Blanc,
Villette,
Louis Bovard 2001,
Switzerland**
Complex flavours of
pineapple, cut grass
and passion-fruit,
well balanced with oak

COLSTEN BASSET STILTON SALAD WITH WALNUTS AND PEAR (serves 4)

INGREDIENTS

POACHING LIQUOR
250 ml dry white wine
250 ml water
1 orange
1 lemon
1 cinnamon stick
2 pears

CREAMED STILTON
200g Colsten Basset stilton
100ml double cream

SALAD
100g crumbled stilton
40g broken walnuts
40g black and white grapes,
halved and deseeded
Lardons of crispy cooked bacon
Sunblush tomatoes
Wild rocket leaves
Salt and pepper

DRESSING
300ml Scrumpy Jack cider
2 tsp Dijon mustard
50ml cider vinegar
50ml olive oil

CHEF'S TIP

Leave out the bacon for a
delicious vegetarian alternative.

METHOD OF PEAR
Thinly peel the rind from the orange and lemon, squeeze the juices
and place in a saucepan with the wine, water and cinnamon. Bring to
the boil and simmer for 15 minutes. Peel the pears, leaving them whole,
place in the poaching liquor and cook until tender. Remove from the
liquor and allow to cool. Cut the pears in half lengthways, remove the
core with a small knife or teaspoon and set aside.

METHOD OF CREAMED STILTON
Crumble the stilton into a mixing bowl, break down with a wooden
spoon and beat until soft. Once soft, slowly add the cream while
continuing to beat. Place the mixture into a piping bag and pipe
into the cavity of each pear half.

METHOD OF DRESSING
Reduce the cider in a small saucepan until it becomes syrupy.
Allow to cool. In a small bowl, whisk together the cider reduction,
the Dijon mustard, and the cider vinegar. Slowly add the olive oil
while continuing to whisk, and season to taste.

METHOD OF SALAD
Place the stilton, walnuts, grapes, bacon, sunblush tomatoes and
rocket in a small mixing bowl. Dress with the cider dressing,
and season to taste.

TO SERVE
Assemble as shown in the photograph, garnishing the pear with a
piece of crisp bacon.

TO DRINK...

**Dry Amontillado,
Barbadillo,
Spain**
Clean and fruity,
full bodied with an
incisive bouquet, and
ample to the palate

TADLEY FOREST VENISON WITH PARSNIP, BLACKBERRIES AND A JUNIPER JUS (serves 4)

INGREDIENTS

PARSNIP PURÉE
5 parsnips
Milk

VENISON SAUCE
1kg chopped venison
bones and trimmings
500g carrots, peeled
and roughly chopped
500g onions, peeled
and roughly chopped
1 bunch thyme
2 bay leaves
20g juniper berries
1 litre chicken stock
1 piece of muslin cloth

STAND-UP PARSNIPS
4 large parsnips
Duck fat

VENISON
4 venison fillets

500g washed spinach to serve
Blackberries to ganish

METHOD OF PARSNIP PURÉE
Peel the tender part of the parsnip and discard the woody root. Cut into 1cm dice and place in a saucepan. Just cover with milk, bring to the boil and cook until tender. Drain, then blend in a food processor until smooth, and set aside.

METHOD OF VENISON SAUCE
In a saucepan, brown the venison bones and trimmings in a little oil, then add the prepared vegetables, herbs and berries. Cook for 10 minutes, then add the chicken stock and simmer for 2 hours. Remove from the heat and strain through a colander lined with muslin into a clean pan. Place back onto the heat and simmer until a light syrupy consistency. Reserve for later.

METHOD OF STAND-UP PARSNIPS
Peel the parsnips, and cut a level slice from the wide end so that they will stand up straight. Place in a saucepan, cover with duck fat and cook gently until tender. Once cooked, remove and drain the parsnips and allow to cool. With a sharp knife carefully cut out the inside of the root and discard. The space will be filled with purée later.

METHOD OF VENISON
Pre-heat the oven to 200°C/400°F/Gas Mark 6. Heat a little oil in an ovenproof pan, add the seasoned venison and lightly colour on all sides. Place the pan in the oven for 2 minutes, then turn the venison over and cook for a further 2 minutes. Remove from the pan, wrap in foil and rest. This length of cooking will give a medium rare result.

TO COOK AND SERVE
Reheat the parsnip purée in a pan. Return the parsnips to the duck fat to reheat. Return the venison to the oven for 2 minutes. Warm the sauce on a low heat. Wilt the spinach over a medium heat with a little butter, and drain on kitchen paper. Place some spinach on a plate, carve each venison fillet diagonally and place on top of spinach. Drain the whole parsnips, fill with purée and stand on the plate. Spoon more purée onto the plate, drizzle with the venison sauce and garnish with blackberries. Serve immediately.

TO DRINK...

Pommard 1er cru Les Croix Noires, Domaine de Courcel, 2000, France
Red fruits and spice characters are balanced by structured tannins and complexity

'TOAD-IN-THE-HOLE' WITH PORK AND APPLE SAUSAGES (serves 4)

INGREDIENTS

YORKSHIRE PUDDING
568ml milk
5 medium eggs
150g plain flour
2 tsp English mustard
Salt and pepper

PEA SAUCE
3 large shallots, finely chopped
300g frozen garden peas
100ml dry white wine
150ml double cream

'TOAD-IN-THE-HOLE'
12 pork and apple sausages
1 dessert apple, peeled and sliced
1 large onion, peeled and sliced
4 sprigs of thyme

VEGETABLES
Carrots, peeled
Celeriac, peeled
Yellow courgette
Green courgette
Raw beetroot, peeled
Shelled peas
Shelled broad beans
Asparagus tips
Butter
Salt and pepper

METHOD OF YORKSHIRE PUDDING BATTER
In a mixing bowl, whisk the eggs and milk together. Slowly whisk in the flour until you have a smooth batter. Season with the English mustard, salt and pepper.

METHOD OF PEA SAUCE
In a saucepan sweat the shallots in a little butter for 2 minutes without letting them take colour. Add the peas, white wine and cream and bring to the boil. Boil for a further 2 minutes (no longer, so as to retain the fresh colour). Place in a liquidiser and purée until smooth. Be careful not to overfill the liquidizer goblet, and risk scalding yourself. Pass through a fine sieve and season to taste.

METHOD OF 'TOAD-IN-THE-HOLE'
Preheat the oven to 200°C/400°F/Gas Mark 6. Heat the olive oil in a frying pan and cook the sausages, turning, until golden brown. Add the apple, onion and thyme and sauté for a further couple of minutes. Place the mixture into either individual moulds or into 1 large mould. Pour the Yorkshire pudding batter over the top and bake in the oven for 30-40 minutes.

METHOD OF VEGETABLES
Cut the first 5 vegetables into small dice (or use a Solferino scoop to make balls). Blanch all the vegetables separately in boiling salted water for a few minutes and refresh in iced water. Set aside. (NB: the beetroot must be blanched separately, otherwise it will bleed into the other vegetables). Once the vegetables have been blanched and chilled, mix them together - except for the beetroot. When the toad-in-the-hole is ready to serve, melt the butter in a pan and warm up the vegetables. Reheat the beetroot separately.

TO SERVE
Cut the toad-in-the-hole into portions, and arrange on a plate with the vegetables and the pea sauce. The dish can be accompanied by mashed potato, or some other potato of your choice.

TO DRINK...

**Merlot, Ronchi
Di Manzano 2003,
Italy**
Layered style
with hints of berry,
plum and mocha,
medium bodied

LIGHTLY POACHED TURBOT WITH CRUMBLED BISCUIT OF HAZELNUT AND OLIVES, FENNEL FOAM *(serves 4)*

INGREDIENTS

TURBOT
1kg turbot, filleted and skinned to yield 4 x 100 to 120g portions
250g butter

FENNEL PURÉE
3 bulbs fennel
112g butter
$^1/_4$pt water

BISCUIT CRUMB
5g cornflour
30g dried olives
15g stale white bread, cut into $^1/_2$ cm dice
30g roasted hazelnuts, whole
25g butter
1 egg white
145ml milk
Large pinch of salt

FENNEL FOAM
330ml double cream
165ml milk
5 tbs fennel purée

VEGETABLE GARNISH
12 baby turnips
4 baby fennel bulbs
8 baby onions

METHOD OF FENNEL PURÉE
Slice the fennel and sauté in butter on a low heat so as not to brown it. Cover with a disc of baking paper. When the fennel is tender, blend to a purée. Set to one side.

METHOD OF BISCUIT CRUMB
Pre-heat the oven to 160°C/310°F/Gas Mark 2. Put the dry ingredients into a bowl, add the melted butter and the remaining ingredients and mix well together. Spread the mixture out on a baking tray. Cook in the oven for 20 minutes, remove from the heat and allow to harden. Once hardened, place in a very heavy-duty polythene bag and crush to a powder with a rolling pin.

METHOD OF FENNEL FOAM
Take 330ml double cream, 165ml milk and 5 tablespoons of fennel purée and bring to the boil. Blend with a hand blender.

METHOD OF VEGETABLE GARNISH
Cook the turnips for 5 minutes in boiling water. Once cooked, run under cold water, peel and reserve. Using fresh water for each vegetable, boil the baby fennel and the baby onions.

TO COOK AND SERVE
Place 250g of butter in a small pan, add 200ml water and warm gently to around 60°C (ie below a simmer). Place the turbot fillets in the pan and poach for 4-5 minutes until tender. Season after cooking. While the fish is cooking, heat the purée and the foam and season. Warm the turnips, the fennel and the onions in salted water. Drain the turbot and sprinkle the crumb liberally over it. Arrange on a plate with the vegetables and foam and serve immediately.

PENNYHILL PARK HOTEL

TO DRINK...

**Meursault,
Pierre André,
1998, France**
Elegant wine
showing honey
characters, displaying
mineral hints

47

RHUBARB AND GINGER CRUMBLE WITH DEVONSHIRE CLOTTED CREAM *(serves 4)*

INGREDIENTS

SWEET PASTRY
100g butter
70g caster sugar
200g plain flour
1¹/₂ whole eggs

GINGER CRUMBLE
200g plain flour
100g butter
100g caster sugar
1 tsp ground ginger

RHUBARB COMPÔTE
100g caster sugar
250g fresh rhubarb
1 vanilla pod
100ml water
25g fresh ginger

RHUBARB BÂTONS
350ml water
350g caster sugar
300g fresh rhubarb
75g fresh raspberries,
pressed through a sieve
to make 50ml raspberry purée

RHUBARB TARTLETS
300g fresh rhubarb
100g caster sugar
15g fresh ginger,
peeled and finely chopped
400g clotted cream Devonshire

METHOD OF SWEET PASTRY
Make the pastry by the rubbing-in method, ie by lightly rubbing the butter cut into small pieces into the flour with your fingertips, until the mixture looks like breadcrumbs. Stir in the sugar, then mix in the beaten eggs. Draw the mixture into a dough with your fingers, and knead lightly until smooth. Chill in the fridge for 20-30 minutes.

METHOD OF CRUMBLE TOPPING
Use the same rubbing-in method to make the crumble, but this time mix the sugar in at the start, and continue rubbing in until the mixture hangs together in small lumps.

METHOD OF RHUBARB COMPÔTE
Peel and chop the ginger, and place with the water, sugar and vanilla pod into a saucepan and bring to the boil. Add the chopped rhubarb and cook to a pulp. Remove from the heat and cool. Remove the vanilla pod when cold.

METHOD OF RHUBARB BÂTONS
Measure the water into a saucepan, add the sugar, and bring to the boil, stirring to dissolve the sugar. Cut the fresh rhubarb into bâtons, 2 inches long by ¹/₂ inch square. Take the syrup off the heat and add the bâtons, and the raspberry purée to colour the rhubarb pink. The rhubarb will slowly cook and soften as the syrup cools. Remove onto kitchen paper when required.

METHOD OF RHUBARB TART
Pre-heat the oven to 200°C/400°F/Gas Mark 6. Wash the rhubarb and cut it up small. Mix together with the fresh ginger and the sugar. Line 4-6 tartlet moulds with the sweet pastry. Put in the rhubarb mixture, and sprinkle the crumble onto the top. Bake in the oven for 20-30 minutes until golden brown.

TO SERVE
Arrange rhubarb bâtons on one third of the plate in a lattice design. Dust a rhubarb tart with icing sugar and place it in the second third of the plate. On the last third of the plate place the compôte. Top with Devonshire clotted cream and finish with a sprig of mint. Drizzle a little of the rhubarb cooking liquid around the plate.

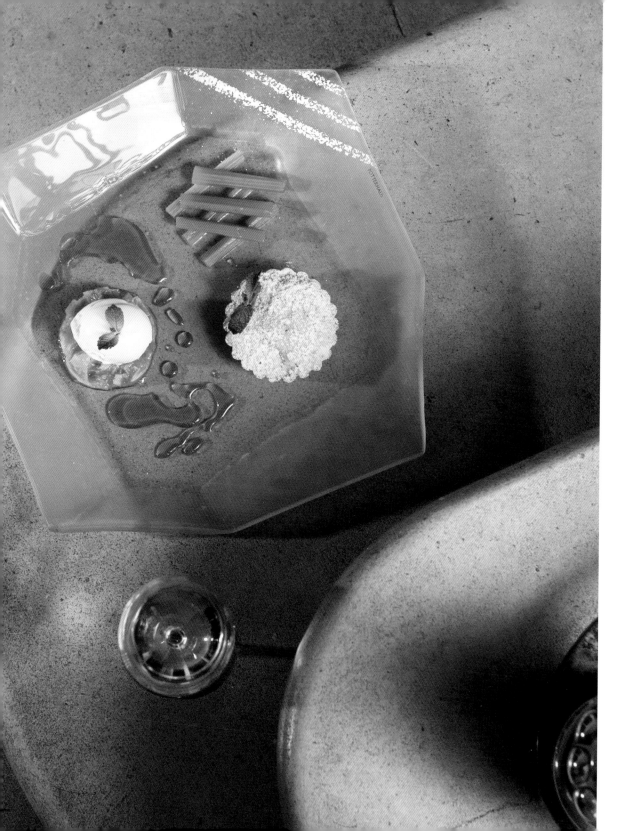

TO DRINK...

Jurançon, La Magendia de Lapeyre, 2002, SW France (sweet white)
Expression of mango, grapefruit and banana bound by crystal-pure acidity

ELDERFLOWER JELLY WITH FRESH BERRIES AND PRESSED RASPBERRIES *(serves 4-6)*

INGREDIENTS

ELDERFLOWER JELLY

125ml elderflower cordial
350ml sparkling water
5$\frac{1}{2}$ gelatine leaves
25g icing sugar
250g fresh raspberries
40g blackberries
75g fresh blueberries
125g fresh strawberries
30g red currants
30g white currants
6 mint tips
Juice of $\frac{1}{4}$ of a lemon

METHOD OF ELDERFLOWER JELLY

Soak the gelatine in a bowl of cold water. Bring the sparkling water to the boil and remove from the heat. Stir in the soaked gelatine and the elderflower cordial, and leave to cool. Pick over the raspberries, blackberries and blueberries, cut up the strawberries, and use a fork to strip the currants off their stalks. Pour jelly into the moulds to one third of the way up and allow to set. Retaining a few berries for the garnish, add some of all of the prepared fruits and 2 leaves of mint to each mould. Pour on another third of jelly to keep the berries in the centre of the mould and allow to set. Then fill the moulds to the top with the remaining jelly and refrigerate.

METHOD OF PRESSED RASPBERRY SAUCE

Mix 150g of raspberries with 25g icing sugar and the lemon juice and pass though a fine sieve into a bowl.

TO SERVE

Remove the jellies from the mould and place onto serving plates and garnish with berries as shown in the photograph. Drizzle a little raspberry sauce around berries on the plates and place one tip of mint on each jelly.

PENNYHILL PARK HOTEL

**Tokaji Cuvée
Kiralyudvar,
Istvan Szepsy,
2000, Hungary
(sweet white)**
Very good balance of
confit fruits, honey
flavours and acidity
with a mineral finish

BAKED VANILLA RICE PUDDING
WITH VICTORIA PLUM COMPÔTE (serves 4)

INGREDIENTS

BAKED RICE PUDDING
1.5 litres milk
2 vanilla pods
300g caster sugar
300g pudding rice

PLUM COMPÔTE
600g Victoria plums
400ml water
200g caster sugar
100g demerara sugar
1/2 cinnamon stick
1 vanilla pod
2 cloves
1 unwaxed lemon
100ml plum wine

METHOD OF BAKED RICE PUDDING
Pre-heat the oven to 200°C/400°F/Gas Mark 6. Pour the milk into a saucepan. Either re-use vanilla pods from which you have already scraped out the seeds for another recipe, or use a new, whole pod; add it to the milk and bring to the boil. Add the rice and the caster sugar. Pour into an ovenproof dish and place in the oven for about 40 minutes or until the rice is cooked. The top should be golden brown and have a skin, which you leave intact. The rice pudding can be served either hot or cold.

METHOD OF PLUM COMPÔTE
Cut the Victoria plums in half and remove the stones. Leaving the white pith behind, cut the yellow part of the peel from a quarter of the lemon, using a very sharp knife or a swivel potato peeler. Measure the water into a saucepan, add the two sugars, the cinnamon stick, the vanilla pod (see previous paragraph), cloves and lemon zest, and bring back to the boil. Add the stoned plums and the plum wine. Cook for 3-4 minutes until the plums have softened. Remove from the heat and cool. When cold, remove the spices and the lemon zest (and reserve for use later as a garnish, if you wish). You may also save 4 plum halves for garnish.

TO COOK AND SERVE
Remove the skin from the rice pudding and cut out 4 rounds from it. Divide the rice pudding into four small dishes and lay a round of skin on top. You may now either reheat the rice pudding or it can be served cold. Serve the plum compôte in four separate small dishes, or serve it on top of the rice pudding, as you wish. Garnish as desired or as shown in the photograph.

TO DRINK...

**Maury, Mas Amiel,
Cuvée Spéciale
10 ans d'age,
France (sweet red)**
Huge bouquet of prune
and plum, combined
with strength,
marvellous elegance
and finesse

Lewis Hamblet
EXECUTIVE CHEF

Years of effort and family support have brought me to South Lodge, working as the Executive Chef. I became passionate about food at a young age. I was brought up in Bolton, and after leaving school I went on to Bolton Metropolitan College where I completed a three-year Catering course.

I went to work at the Savoy Hotel in London, then two years later I moved to Amberley Castle, and from there to The Manor House.

It was whilst working there that I met my future wife Haley. We married in 1997, and have three children: Tom, Charlie and Beth. In 1994 I won the Kitchen section of the Annual Awards of Excellence of the Academy of Culinary Arts and that's how I gained the position of senior sous chef at The Manor House.

I spent six years at The Manor House and have now been working at South Lodge for eight years. South Lodge has been constantly evolving and expanding throughout my time here.

Winning the Academy in 1994 and also keeping the 3 rosettes have been my professional achievements. I feel very proud of myself and proud of the way my children are developing and myself being able to support their comfortable upbringing.

I feel inspired by my surroundings, seeing different produce - even walking round a farmers' market can inspire me. I don't always get inspiration from other chefs although I do admire Gary Rhodes and Marco Pierre White. I feel inspiration from people I meet in everyday life on the street, a comment they make may strike a chord within me and I react to it in the kitchen.

When I'm cooking I feel completely at home. I like to use good seasonal local produce and cook simply, taking care not to detract from the main ingredients. Cooking has been my life, it's important to me, along with my family. If I am not cooking I'm either at home with my family or out running. I hope my recipes will inspire you to get passionate about food, please enjoy!

South Lodge Hotel

MENU

SAUTÉED SQUID RINGS
with bell peppers, chorizo

LAYERED CRAB, AVOCADO AND TOMATO
antibes dressing (sauce antiboise), basil tempura

SAUTÉED LAMBS KIDNEYS
roasted red onion, parsnip risotto, madeira jus

ROASTED PIGEON
*with nutmeg spätzle, red cabbage,
sweet potato purée and a wine sauce*

STEAMED SALMON
char-roasted vegetables, pak choi, saffron dressing

VANILLA ROASTED GRESSINGHAM DUCK
*caramelised chicory, orange and
pomegranate reduction*

CLASSIC APPLE TARTE TATIN
with clotted cream

PINEAPPLE FINANCIER
coconut sorbet, roasted pineapple compôte

CHOCOLATE AND SUMMER FRUIT SUNDAE
with a crunchy honeycomb topping

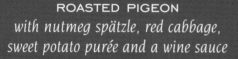

The Camellia Restaurant

SAUTÉED SQUID RINGS WITH BELL PEPPERS AND CHORIZO *(serves 4)*

INGREDIENTS

2 medium squid tubes
1 red pepper
1 green pepper
1 yellow pepper
150g good quality chorizo
1 lemon
Olive oil
Balsamic vinegar
Salt and pepper

METHOD OF SQUID

Clean the squid tubes by pulling off any skin and attached bits, and rinse under cold water. Slice into rings. Grate the zest of the lemon and set aside. Cut the peppers into four from the stalk down. Remove the seeds and white membrane, and cut the peppers into thin strips. Cut the chorizo into slices about 5mm thick.

TO COOK AND SERVE

Heat some olive oil in a frying pan about 10 in/25 cm wide. Fry the chorizo for about 30 seconds on each side or until it begins to colour. Remove and keep warm. Put the peppers into the pan and cook until they begin to soften slightly. Remove and keep warm. Fry the squid for 1 minute, squeeze in a little lemon juice, season and remove. Build the peppers, chorizo and squid up onto a plate, drizzle with olive oil and balsamic vinegar and serve with the lemon zest sprinkled over.

TO DRINK...

**Gran Vina Sol
Chardonnay,
Miguel Torres 2003**
An oaky chardonnay
from Spain with light
fragrance and acidity
still present

LAYERED CRAB, AVOCADO AND TOMATO WITH ANTIBES DRESSING (SAUCE ANTIBOISE), BASIL TEMPURA (*serves* 4)

INGREDIENTS

CRAB
1 whole crab
1 avocado
2 plum tomatoes
1 lemon
1 small bunch chives

DRESSING
10 black and 10 green olives
50g sunblush tomatoes
4 spring onions
. Olive oil
4 basil leaves

METHOD OF CRAB
Either boil or steam the crab for 14 minutes. Remove the claws, break them open, and carefully pick out the white meat. Check that there are no small pieces of shell in it, and keep to one side. Peel the avocado, remove the stone and dice the flesh. Add a little lemon juice to stop it going brown and lightly season. Cut a little cross at the top of the tomatoes, put them into boiling water for 10 seconds, then put them into very cold water. Remove the skin, cut each tomato into four, scoop out the seeds and core, and dice the flesh. Chop the chives and add to the white crab meat.

METHOD OF DRESSING
Cut the olives and tomatoes into pieces roughly the same size. Peel the outer layer of skin from the spring onions, and slice them thinly. Put all of the above into enough olive oil to bind them together.

TO COMPLETE AND SERVE
Using a tall ring or cutter, build up the crab, avocado and tomato into a stack on each plate. Spoon the dressing around. Dip the basil leaves into hot oil for 5 seconds and place on top of the crab. (If the ingredients are stacked up in the order described, the basil tempura will be going on top of the tomato).

TO DRINK...

**Gewrüztraminer
A. Sherer 2002**
A very aromatic
wine, with complexity
(fruity, flowery, spicy)
and no acidity

63

SAUTÉED LAMBS KIDNEYS WITH ROASTED RED ONION, PARSNIP RISOTTO, MADEIRA JUS (*serves* 4)

INGREDIENTS

6 lamb's kidneys

2 red onions
(peeled and cut into quarters)

2 parsnips *(peeled and cut up)*

100ml white wine

50g risotto rice *(Arborio)*

1 shallot

2 sprigs thyme
(pick the leaves from the stalk of one,
use the other to garnish)

Knob of butter

Olive oil

1 chicken or vegetable
stock cube

¹/₂ pint chicken stock

50ml Madeira

METHOD OF SAUCE

In the kitchen at South Lodge we make our sauces from bone reductions. This is a long process, taking up to a couple of days. In the home environment you can make the sauce by reducing some chicken stock, thickening it with a little cornflour, then adding some Madeira at the end.

METHOD OF RISOTTO

Boil the parsnips until soft in enough water to cover. Drain off the cooking liquid and retain it and the parsnips. Measure the white wine and add the parsnip cooking liquid until you have 300ml. Dice the shallot and cook it slowly with the thyme leaves, butter and olive oil until soft, making sure that you do not allow it to colour. Add the rice, and stir for a couple of minutes. Then add the parsnip liquid a little at a time until it has all been absorbed. This process will take about 15 minutes - the rice should offer only a little resistance when tasted. Add the parsnips and season to taste.

METHOD OF RED ONIONS

Pre-heat the oven to 200°C/400°F/Gas Mark 6. Toss the quartered onions in olive oil and roast them on a shallow tray for 45 minutes, turning once.

METHOD OF KIDNEYS

Season the kidneys, brown them in a pan with a little oil, then cook in the hot oven for about 4 minutes. Allow them to rest for two minutes after you take them out of the oven.

TO SERVE

Place some of the risotto in each bowl, and spoon the sauce around. Slice the kidneys in half lengthways and arrange three halves per portion on the risotto, with two quarters of red onion alongside. Garnish with a sprig of thyme if available.

TO DRINK...

Château les Bertrands 2004, Premières Côtes de Blaye, Bordeaux
A blend of semillon and sauvignon blanc, easy drinking and fruity

65

The Camellia Restaurant

ROASTED PIGEON, WITH NUTMEG SPÄTZLE, RED CABBAGE, SWEET POTATO PURÉE AND A WINE SAUCE *(serves 4)*

INGREDIENTS

PIGEON
4 oven ready pigeons

SWEET POTATO PURÉE
750g sweet potatoes

RED CABBAGE
400g finely shredded
red cabbage
1 grated apple
1 small onion, diced
100ml orange juice
100ml water
1 tbs redcurrant jelly

WINE SAUCE
1 wine glass red wine
1 wine glass port
100ml chicken stock
1 shallot, sliced
Sprig of thyme
50ml double cream
100g unsalted butter

SPÄTZLE
200g plain flour
5 eggs
1/4 tsp grated nutmeg

METHOD OF RED CABBAGE
Place all the ingredients in a saucepan, and cover with a circle of greaseproof paper, but no lid. Cook slowly for about 1 hour on the top of the cooker on a medium heat, until most of the liquid has been absorbed, lifting the paper off and stirring to prevent sticking.

METHOD OF WINE SAUCE
Pour the wine, port and stock into a pan, add the sliced shallot and sprig of thyme, and boil to reduce by three quarters. Add a little cream, bring to the boil again, then whisk in 100g butter and keep warm (once the butter has been added, do not re-boil the sauce).

METHOD OF SPÄTZLE
Mix all the ingredients together, season, and thin with a little water so the mixture is not too thick. Push the mixture through a colander into a pan of boiling water and poach for 2 minutes. Strain, cool and set aside.

METHOD OF SWEET POTATO PURÉE
Peel, cut up and boil the sweet potatoes in salted water. Mash with a little butter, season, and keep warm.

TO COOK AND SERVE
Preheat the oven to 200°C/400°F/Gas Mark 6. Season and brown the pigeons in a frying-pan, then roast them for 10 minutes. Allow to rest for 3 minutes before proceeding. Reheat the red cabbage, and spoon onto the serving plate. Reheat the spätzle with a little butter and place on the plate in a ring.
To remove the pigeon breasts, slice along the breast bone with a sharp knife, continue slicing over the ribcage staying as close to the bone as possible, detach the breasts and sit them on top of the red cabbage. Place some sweet potato purée on the plate, whisk the wine sauce and add a pool of it to the plate (or drizzle it over the contents of the plate, or use according to your preference) and serve immediately.

TO DRINK...

**Château Pichon
Longueville Comtesse
de Lalande,
2eme cru classé
Pauillac 1993**
Deep in colour, rich
and intense on the
palate. Powerful, ripe
blackcurrant flavours
balanced by classy oak

STEAMED SALMON, CHAR-ROASTED VEGETABLES, PAK CHOI SAFFRON DRESSING (*serves* 4)

INGREDIENTS

4 x 150g fillets of salmon
4 heads pak choi
1 red pepper
1 yellow pepper
1 green pepper
1 aubergine
1 large courgette
2 cloves garlic
1 lemon
4 shallots
200ml good olive oil
1g saffron
25ml white wine vinegar

METHOD

Remove the stalk at the bottom of the pak choi and discard. Put the leaves into boiling water for 30 seconds, remove and cool under running water and set aside. Remove the stalk from each pepper, cut in half, scrape out and discard the seeds, and cut each half pepper into 4 pieces. Slice the aubergine across into 8 slices, and do the same with the courgette. Drizzle a little olive oil onto a ridged grill pan, heat steadily until hot and cook the above vegetables until they take on the lined markings from the pan (1 to 2 minutes each side). Place the grilled vegetables in an ovenproof dish, season, add rosemary, thyme and olive oil, leaving 100ml for the sauce. Roast in a hot oven for about 10 minutes. For the sauce, dice the shallots and sweat them in a little of the olive oil. Add the saffron, stir for a couple of minutes, and then add the rest of the olive oil and the vinegar. Cook slowly for about 20 minutes. Season the salmon and steam it for 8 minutes. When cooked, squeeze on a little lemon juice.

TO SERVE

Warm through the pak choi, place the salmon on top, distribute the char-grilled vegetables around the outside and drizzle the dressing around.

SOUTH LODGE HOTEL

TO DRINK...

Meursault 1er Cru 1998
This chardonnay from Burgundy has lost its acidity to become a rich, buttery and opulent wine

69

VANILLA ROASTED GRESSINGHAM DUCK WITH CARAMELISED CHICORY, ORANGE AND POMEGRANATE REDUCTION (*serves* 4)

INGREDIENTS

4 duck breasts
(*I prefer to use Gressingham,
but any duck can be used*)
1 vanilla pod
Light brush of olive oil

SAUCE

2 tbs demerara sugar
100ml orange juice
2 oranges
1 pomegranate

VEGETABLE GARNISH

2 large potatoes,
peeled and grated
1 egg
50g flour
2 heads Belgian chicory
1 x 250g bag of
washed spinach

METHOD OF VEGETABLE GARNISH

Mix together the grated potato, egg and flour, season, and roll into balls the size of a golf ball. Deep-fry until golden. Remove the outside leaves from the chicory, slice in half lengthways, and cook slowly in a little oil or butter on each side for about 20 minutes until soft and golden in colour. A light sprinkling of sugar will help the browning process. Season and keep warm. Put the spinach into a saucepan with a knob of butter and a splash of water, place a lid on the pan and cook for 2 minutes.

METHOD OF DUCK

Pre-heat the oven to 200°C/400°F/Gas Mark 6. Split the vanilla pod lengthways, scrape out the seeds and spread them over the skin side of each duck breast, keeping the vanilla pod for use in another recipe. Season the duck and brown on all sides in a pan before roasting in a hot oven for about ten minutes for juicy and rare, or longer if you prefer it well done. Remove the duck from the oven and allow it to rest.

METHOD OF SAUCE

Tip the excess duck fat out of the pan, add the sugar and place on a medium to low heat to melt the sugar. Once the sugar begins to turn a golden colour, add the orange juice and the vanilla pod. Whilst this is reducing to a syrupy consistency, slice the peel and skin off the oranges with a sharp knife and lever out the segments (leaving the skin behind). Cut open the pomegranate and remove the seeds. Once the sauce is reduced by half, add to it the orange segments and the pomegranate seeds.

TO SERVE

Slice the duck lengthways into about 6 slices per breast and lay it over the chicory Put a little pile of spinach onto each plate and place the potato on top. Spoon on the sauce, taking care to distribute the fruit evenly.

TO DRINK...

Château Musar 1998, Lebanon
This wine is a blend of cabernet, cinsault and carignan and has the body and the acidity to complement this dish

CLASSIC APPLE TARTE TATIN
WITH CLOTTED CREAM *(serves 4)*

INGREDIENTS

4 good quality dessert
apples, such as Braeburn
30g unsalted butter
50g castor sugar
100g good quality
ready-made puff pastry
Clotted cream

Selection of summer
berries for garnish

CHEF'S TIP

This is best served hot,
with the clotted cream
melting on top.

METHOD OF TARTE TATIN

Pre-heat the oven to 190°C/375°F/Gas Mark 5. Peel and core the apples and cut in half. Set to one side. Roll the puff pastry out evenly to a thickness of about 2mm, and prick all over with a fork. Using a fairly shallow 8in/20cm metal pan as a template, cut the pastry so as to obtain a disc that is about 2.5cm bigger all round than the pan. Distribute the butter and sugar evenly over the bottom of the pan. Next, lay the apple halves evenly on top, cut side up, and finally cover with the puff pastry, folding the excess pastry under the apples. Place the pan on a fairly high heat to start to caramelise the apples. This should take about 5-10 minutes, but keep checking the apples by gently lifting the pastry. Once the apples have taken colour, finish the tart by baking in the oven until the pastry is golden brown.

TO SERVE

When you take the tart out of the oven, place a serving plate over it and invert it so that the pastry is on the bottom of the serving plate and the caramelised apples on top. Using a wet, warm tablespoon, scoop some clotted cream on top and garnish with the berries.

SOUTH LODGE HOTEL

TO DRINK...

**Monbazillac 1997
Château Dech
la Calevie**
This dessert requires
a wine with a bit of
acidity but with
richness as well

PINEAPPLE FINANCIER, COCONUT SORBET, ROAST PINEAPPLE COMPÔTE *(serves 4)*

INGREDIENTS

ROAST PINEAPPLE
1 large pineapple
50g brown sugar
1 tsp ground star anise
1 tsp ground mixed spice
220g sugar syrup
*(110g water and 110g
sugar boiled together)*

SORBET
500ml coconut milk
180g sugar
20g glucose
25ml Malibu coconut liqueur

FINANCIER
6 egg whites
150g icing sugar
75g ground almonds
50g plain cake flour
Zest of 2 lemons
125g butter
1 vanilla pod

Small sprigs of
rosemary to garnish

METHOD OF PINEAPPLE
Pre-heat the oven to 150ºC/300ºF/Gas Mark 2. Remove the skin from the pineapple, making sure you remove the 'eyes' of the fruit. Cut down either side of the core, giving you 2 large sides and 2 small sides of pineapple. Trim all 4 pieces so that all the sides are flat, then cut 3 pieces into batons (reserving the fourth piece for the bottom of your financier). Roll the batons in sugar and spice, place in an oven dish and roast in the oven for 15 minutes, turning half way through. They will take on some of the colour of the sugar. Once they are cooked, leave aside to cool. Dice the reserved piece of pineapple and cook on a low heat in the sugar syrup for 10 minutes. Drain and cool.

METHOD OF SORBET
Bring all 4 ingredients to a boil and remove from the heat. Chill the mixture in the fridge. Once cold, either place in a plastic container and freeze, stirring with a fork every 45 minutes or, if you have one, churn in an ice cream machine.

METHOD OF FINANCIER
Beat together the egg whites, icing sugar, ground almonds and flour until really smooth. Add the grated lemon zest. Split the vanilla pod and scrape out the seeds. In a small saucepan heat the butter with the vanilla seeds until it is brown and releases a nutty aroma. Allow the butter to cool, then fold it into the egg mixture and leave to rest for 10 minutes. Grease 4 individual rings with butter or non-stick spray and place on a baking tray. Place some of the diced pineapple in the bottom of each ring, and cover with the egg mixture to 1cm below the top. Bake for 40 minutes in the pre-heated oven, then remove and allow to cool for 10 minutes.

TO SERVE
In the bottom of the plate arrange batons in stacks of 3; place the financier in the opposite corner, and the sorbet on top. Garnish with rosemary and drizzled syrup.

TO DRINK...

**Muscat de Beaumes
de Venise 2001**
A very perfumed
wine, with exotic
and lemony flavours,
rich and with a
long aftertaste

CHOCOLATE AND SUMMER FRUIT SUNDAE WITH A CRUNCHY HONEYCOMB TOPPING (*serves* 4)

INGREDIENTS

CHOCOLATE SAUCE
125g water
75g sugar
25g cocoa powder
25g glucose
25g chocolate

CHOCOLATE BROWNIE
300g sugar
5 eggs
100g flour
35g cocoa powder
500g butter
500g dark chocolate
100g white chocolate buttons

HONEYCOMB
225g sugar
300ml water
25g golden syrup
15ml warm water
$^1/_2$ tsp cream of tartar
$^1/_2$ tsp bicarbonate of soda

SUMMER FRUITS
Strawberries (*hulled*)
A selection of other summer fruits

METHOD OF CHOCOLATE SAUCE
Place the first 4 ingredients in a saucepan and bring to the boil. Once the mixture has boiled, turn down the heat and leave to bubble gently for 15 minutes. Then add the chocolate. Cool, then refrigerate.

METHOD OF CHOCOLATE BROWNIE
Pre-heat the oven to 180°C/350°F/Gas Mark 4. Melt the butter, add the chocolate and stir until the chocolate has fully melted. In a bowl, whisk together the eggs and the sugar until the ribbon stage is reached (the mixture will hold the trail of a figure of eight). Fold in the flour and the cocoa, then the melted butter and chocolate mixture, and finally the white chocolate buttons. Line a baking tray with silicone/greaseproof paper, pour in the mixture and bake for 20 minutes Remove from the oven and put to chill straight away.

METHOD OF HONEYCOMB
Place the sugar, water, golden syrup and cream of tartar into a heavy saucepan. Heat until the sugar has completely dissolved. Boil the mixture without stirring to 154°C on a sugar thermometer, then remove from the heat to prevent further cooking. Quickly mix the bicarbonate into the warm water and add to the hot sugar mixture, stirring carefully. Pour the mixture into a non-stick tray 7in x 11in/18cm x 28cm, and allow to cool. Break into pieces when cold.

TO SERVE
Place a layer of strawberries at the bottom of a glass sundae dish, then layer up a selection of berries, pieces of brownie, and 2 scoops of good quality vanilla ice cream. Cover with the chocolate sauce and garnish with the broken honeycomb.

SOUTH LODGE HOTEL

TO DRINK...

Weltevrede Cape Muscat, origin Robertson
A red dessert wine, powerful and rich in alcohol, will cut the bitterness of the chocolate

David Campbell
EXECUTIVE CHEF

My interest in food started at a young age. I was brought up with my aunt and my gran, who both were fantastic home cooks. My aunt would always have something cooking, whether it be a stock simmering away or a casserole slowly ticking over. At Christmas she would prepare truffles and marzipans, make a cake or be stuffing a turkey, so my radar, which is and always has been alerted by the smell of food, was set from quite an early age. I would ask questions, stick my fingers in things and generally be a nuisance, but I was hooked. I decided from about 12 that I was to be a chef!

My family had quite a history of catering running through it, my uncle had worked his way through the kitchens of some of Britain's largest, busiest and best hotels. From here he had progressed to management and was the general manager of a beautiful hotel in Sutton Coldfield. We would often have family gatherings there, I was seduced by the glamour of it all, people in tuxedos, waiters filleting Dover soles at the table, bell boys carting luggage in and out of cars. My uncle took me on a tour of his kitchen when I was 15, I was mesmerised and knew straight away that this was where I would spend my life.

I left school at sixteen and started a three-year apprenticeship in Glasgow with Jaques Molinari, he was an old-school French chef who had been working in kitchens from the age of 12, and his depth of knowledge and understanding of his trade was an inspiration to me. I spent three years with him before moving to London; after spells at the Ritz, the Chelsea on Sloane Street and the Gallery Hotel I moved to Camberley and Pennyhill Park, where I worked as senior sous chef for seven eventful years. It was here I began working with the England rugby team, I was team chef for their summer tours and was invited by Sir Clive Woodward to join them on their bid to become world champions. The rest, as they say, is history!!

I have been Executive Chef at The Manor House now for one year, it is a fantastic property and it allows me to express my style of food, I have found my nirvana!

In what spare time I have I will be watching sport on telly or down at the gym keeping fit. Eating out is a passion as well and I try to get out about twice a month.

The Manor House Hotel and Golf Club

MENU

THE MANOR HOUSE
HOTEL AND GOLF CLUB

WILTSHIRE BRAWN
*with pickled red onion rings
and grilled rosemary bread*

SAUTÉ OF CRISP LOCAL LAMBS SWEETBREADS
*with summer pea purée, cider and bacon
dressing scented with tarragon*

SCRAMBLED HENS EGGS
with cornish crab and lemon

BARN RAISED CORN FED CHICKEN
*with carrots in a sultana
and coriander broth*

GRILLED RED MULLET ON
CRUSHED WILD POTATOES
with niçoise garnish, bitter salad leaves

SAUTÉ OF QUAIL
with goats cheese and thyme risotto

ROSEMARY PANNA COTTA
with cherry crumble

STRAWBERRY PAVLOVA

SCONES

WILTSHIRE BRAWN WITH PICKLED RED ONION RINGS AND GRILLED ROSEMARY BREAD *(serves 4)*

INGREDIENTS

POACHING STOCK

1 pig's head
6 carrots
6 onions
4 leeks
2 heads celery
4 sprigs rosemary
4 sprigs thyme
1 bulb garlic
2 ham hocks
20g coriander seed
1 cinnamon stick
2 star anise

CIDER REDUCTION

20 shallots
6 sprigs rosemary
6 sprigs thyme
50ml cider vinegar
1 litre dry cider

METHOD OF POACHING STOCK

Soak the pig's head in cold water for 24 hours. Remove, dry with a cloth and discard the water. Burn off all the hairs with a blowtorch. Add to a very large saucepan with all the other stock ingredients, and cover with water. Simmer for about 4 hours, or until the meat is falling off the bone. Remove the head from the stock, and drain. Strain the stock through a fine sieve, return it to the saucepan, and boil to reduce to approximately 1 litre. Wearing rubber gloves (essential), separate the four different elements of the pig's head: Remove the brain, and dice it into 1cm cubes. Chop the 2 pig's cheeks into strips 2cm wide by 1cm, cutting at an angle to make diamond or lozenge shapes. Break the sweetbreads into little nuggets. Cut the tongue into julienne strips. Also cut the ham hock into strips 2cm x 1cm, like the cheeks. Refrigerate for an hour or so until the meats firm up.

METHOD OF CIDER REDUCTION

Finely chop the shallots. Strip the leaves from the stalks and finely chop the herbs, discarding the stalks. Sweat the shallots and herbs with a little olive oil on a low heat until soft, taking care that they do not colour. Add the cider vinegar and the cider and reduce to a syrupy consistency, about 100ml. Now add the pork stock, and bring the combined liquids to the boil. Take a cup for each person and half fill with meat, then pour in the hot stock. Allow to cool, and refrigerate for about 6 hours until set.

TO SERVE

Turn each little mould out onto a serving plate (dip into very hot water for a second or two to loosen). Garnish with pickled red onion rings, and serve with grilled rosemary bread or toasted ciabatta.

TO DRINK...

**Pouilly Fuissé,
Domaine Delorme,
France, 2002**
Mineral finesse
supported by mild
creamy oakiness

SAUTÉ OF CRISP LOCAL LAMB SWEETBREADS WITH SUMMER PEA PURÉE, CIDER AND BACON DRESSING SCENTED WITH TARRAGON *(serves 4)*

INGREDIENTS

SWEETBREADS
500g lambs' sweetbreads
1 litre chicken stock
1 carrot
1 celery stick
1 small leek
1 lemon
2 sprigs thyme
1 bay leaf
1 teaspoon white peppercorns

PEA PURÉE
500g fresh shelled English peas
1/2 litre chicken stock
1 sprig mint
Black pepper
Sea salt

CIDER AND BACON DRESSING
100ml walnut oil
35ml cider vinegar
4 rashers of rindless
smoked back bacon
50g fresh shelled English peas
Tarragon
2 peeled plum tomatoes
Black pepper
Sea salt

Pea shoots to garnish

METHOD OF SWEETBREADS
Place the sweetbreads in a bowl and run them under cold water until almost white in colour (or ask your butcher to do this for you). Peel and roughly dice the vegetables, and place in a saucepan with the chicken stock, the whole lemon, herbs and peppercorns. Bring to the boil. Add the sweetbreads to the boiling chicken stock, turn the heat down and simmer gently for five minutes. Remove from the heat and drain the sweetbreads. When cool enough to handle, remove any excess fat and gristle and discard this along with the stock.

METHOD OF PEA PURÉE
Bring the chicken stock to the boil with the mint, pepper and sea salt, add the peas and cook for 4 minutes. Place in a food processor and process on high speed until smooth.

METHOD OF CIDER AND BACON DRESSING
Place walnut oil, cider vinegar and tarragon in a food processor and blitz. To peel the tomatoes, remove the stalk and make a shallow cross cut in the skin, then blanch for 10 seconds in fast boiling water. Plunge immediately into ice cold water and drain. Remove the skin with a small knife. Cut the tomatoes into quarters; remove the seeds and fibrous core, drain, and dice the flesh into small squares.

TO COOK AND SERVE
In a hot, non-stick frying pan, sauté the diced bacon until crisp, add the sweetbreads and cook for 1 minute on a high heat, turning carefully. Reduce the heat to low; add most of the cider and walnut vinaigrette, the diced tomato and the fresh peas, and season; it is intended to retain the crunchy texture of the peas. Place a tablespoon of the pea purée in the centre of each bowl. Place sweetbreads and bacon mix on the purée, and drizzle a little reserved dressing around the bowl. Garnish the top with pea shoots (or with narrow strips of mangetout if pea shoots are not available).

TO DRINK...

Parès Balta, Blanc le Pacs, Spain, 2004
Aromatic wine made with Xarel.Lo, Parellada and Macabeo grapes. Pear and apples and freshness on the palate

SCRAMBLED HENS EGGS WITH
CORNISH CRAB AND LEMON (*serves* 4)

INGREDIENTS

CRAB SCRAMBLE

8 hen's eggs
(*sourced from a local farm*)
1/2 pint double cream
1 large cock crab
100g chives
Salt and pepper
Chervil to garnish

LEMON CONFIT

2 large lemons
200ml water
200g caster sugar
1 stick cinnamon
1 star anise

MELBA TOAST

4 slices of white organic bread,
cut to a medium thickness

CHEF'S TIP

If you really want to impress at
a dinner party, add a dollop of
caviar on top of the egg as well
as the lemon confit. This adds a
touch of elegance to the dish and
the salt from the caviar works
beautifully with the egg.

METHOD OF CRAB SCRAMBLE

Poach the crab in boiling water for 11 minutes. Remove from the heat,
drain and chill. Remove the claws from the shell and crack using a
household hammer. Pick the flesh from the shell onto a metal tray.
Press the flesh against the tray with the back of a fork, making sure
all the shell is removed. Finely chop the chives. Crack the eggs into
a bowl and whisk.

METHOD OF LEMON CONFIT

Put the water, sugar, cinnamon and star anise into a pan and bring to the
boil. Simmer for one hour. Zest the lemons and add to the stock syrup.
Leave to infuse for one hour, and then drain and discard the stock syrup,
retaining only the lemon zest.

METHOD OF MELBA TOAST

Toast the bread on both sides. Cool for one minute. Take a sharp carving
knife and split the slice of toast through the centre. Place the uncooked
side flat on a table and rub the excess bread crumbs off. Turn it over, cut
into triangles and place under a hot grill until the toast curls at the edges.

TO COOK AND SERVE

In a heavy-based pan, bring the cream to the boil and reduce by one
third. Add the eggs, stirring constantly until they just start to set.
Remove from the heat. Add the crab and the chives. Place back on the
heat for approximately 20 seconds stirring all the time. Season with salt
and pepper and quickly transfer into four bowls. Place approximately
1/2 teaspoon of the lemon confit on top of the scrambled egg and garnish
with a sprig of chervil. Place the Melba toast onto four side plates.

TO DRINK...

Chablis 1er Cru Vaucoupin, Alain Gautheron, France, 2004
Splendid example of Chablis with citrus notes well balanced with oak and minerality

BARN RAISED CORN FED CHICKEN WITH CARROTS IN A SULTANA AND CORIANDER BROTH *(serves 4)*

INGREDIENTS

CORN FED CHICKEN

4 free range organic
chicken breasts
300ml dark chicken stock
200ml dry white wine
2 sprigs of thyme
100g unsalted butter
1 bunch of coriander
Olive oil for frying
Salt and pepper

CARROTS

32 baby bunched carrots

SULTANAS

250g sultanas
200ml white port
Honey to taste
1 vanilla pod

BEETROOT

2 whole raw beetroot
Vegetable oil

CHEF'S TIP

Use the best chicken available.
It's a simple dish with only
three main components.

METHOD OF CORN FED CHICKEN

Pre-heat oven to 200°C/400°F/Gas Mark 6. Season the chicken breasts on both sides with salt and pepper. Seal in a hot ovenproof pan with half the butter and a touch of olive oil, and the thyme. Add the white wine and dark chicken stock. Turn the chicken skin side up and place the pan in the oven for 10 minutes. Remove chicken and reserve. Strain the cooking liquor through a fine sieve into a pan and add the remainder of the butter. Boil rapidly until the liquid has reduced by two thirds. Set aside.

METHOD OF CARROTS

Trim the carrots to leave about an inch of green stalk, peel them, and blanch in boiling water for 1 minute.

METHOD OF SULTANAS

Combine the sultanas with the white port and honey. Split the vanilla pod and scrape the seeds into the sultana mix. Cover with cling film and leave in a warm place until the sultanas have absorbed all the liquid.

METHOD OF BEETROOT

Put on a pair of rubber gloves to peel the beetroot, using a small knife. With a very sharp knife, thinly slice the beetroot and then cut into thin strips or julienne (the beetroot should resemble fine string). Warm the oil in a pan to 140 degrees, drop the beetroot into the oil and take care, as the beetroot will bubble. When the bubbles have stopped it means the water has come out and the beetroot is ready, so remove onto draining paper, season and set aside.

TO COOK AND SERVE

Place the carrots in the chicken cooking liquor and bring to a rapid boil, add the sultanas and cook for 1 min. Chop the coriander finely, add to the sauce and check the seasoning. Cut each chicken breast into three lengthways strips and return to the pan to warm through with the carrots and sultanas for approx 45 seconds. To serve, place 8 carrots neatly into the centre of each bowl, place three strips of chicken on top, spoon the sauce around and over the chicken and top with a neat pile of the beetroot.

THE MANOR HOUSE
HOTEL AND GOLF CLUB

TO DRINK...

**Beaujolais Villages,
Domaine Gry-Sablon,
France, 2004**
Light-bodied red wine
with red fruit flavours

91

GRILLED RED MULLET ON WILD POTATOES, NIÇOISE GARNISH, BITTER SALAD LEAVES *(serves 4)*

INGREDIENTS

MULLET

4 x 200g fillets of red mullet,
de-scaled, pin bones removed
(*ask your fishmonger to do it*)
Knob of butter

CRUSHED POTATOES

600g of wild potatoes
(*speak to your local
vegetable supplier to source*).
If not available, choose
Jersey Royals or
French La Ratte potatoes.
100g unsalted butter
1 bunch of basil, picked
and shredded finely
just before using

NIÇOISE GARNISH

10 French beans
2 plum tomatoes
8 large sweet green olives
8 quail's eggs
Vinegar (*any type*)
4 pieces of baby fennel
Extra virgin olive oil to dress

BITTER SALAD

Baby oak leaf
Coarse frisée
Baby gem lettuce
Bitter Baby cos

METHOD OF CRUSHED POTATOES

Wash the potatoes, and boil in salted water until cooked. Drain, cool, and peel using a small sharp knife. Warm the butter gently in a pan. Add the potatoes and crush with a fork until they are broken down but not mashed. Season with salt and pepper. Add the basil and keep warm.

METHOD OF NIÇOISE GARNISH

Bring a large saucepan of water to the boil. Season with salt. Remove the coarse stalk from the French beans. Trim the baby fennel. Blanch the beans and the fennel together until *al dente*. Drain and set aside. To peel the tomato, remove the stalk and make a shallow cross cut in the skin, then blanch for 10 seconds in fast boiling water. Plunge immediately into ice cold water and drain. Remove the skin with a small knife. Cut the tomato into quarters; remove the seeds and fibrous core to leave four petals. Cut the ends from the olives so they sit up. Poach quail eggs in water with a tablespoon of vinegar until soft. Drain and set aside.

METHOD OF BITTER SALAD

Wash and pick over the leaves, tear into small pieces and set aside.

TO COOK AND SERVE

Season the red mullet fillets with salt and pepper and place in a very hot non-stick frying pan with a touch of olive oil and a knob of butter. Gently shake the pan to ensure the mullet does not stick. After one minute gently turn the fillets over using a fish slice. Cook for a further 30 seconds, then remove from the pan. Warm the beans and fennel. Place the potatoes into four even sized rings in the centre of the plate. Place the mullet on top. Arrange the fennel, beans, tomato petals and quail eggs around the potato and mullet. Place two olives per plate. Dress the salad leaves with salt and a little olive oil and arrange on the plate. Drizzle the plate with a little more olive oil.

THE MANOR HOUSE
HOTEL AND GOLF CLUB

TO DRINK...

Gavi di Gavi, Masseria di Carmelitani, Italy, 2004
Rich and full flavours of fruit over floral notes, dry and crisp on the palate, full and deep with finesse

SAUTÉ OF QUAIL WITH GOATS CHEESE AND THYME RISOTTO (*serves* 4)

INGREDIENTS

QUAIL
4 quails

ORANGE CONFIT
2 oranges
200ml water
200g caster sugar
1 stick cinnamon
1 star anise

QUAIL STOCK
1 carrot
1 leek
1 small onion
2 sprigs of thyme
White peppercorns,
black peppercorns

RISOTTO
2 cloves of garlic, chopped
300g Arborio risotto rice
2 shallots, finely chopped
10 sprigs of thyme, leaves picked off
2 *crottins Chavignols* goats cheese
50g unsalted butter
Olive oil
300ml dry white wine

Pea shoots to garnish
Confit orange zest to garnish

METHOD OF QUAIL STOCK
Clean, trim and wash the leek, then roughly chop; peel and roughly chop the carrot and onion, and sweat the vegetables together in a pan with a little oil. Deglaze the pan with red wine, add the quail legs and caramelise. Add 1 litre of cold water and bring slowly to the boil, skimming off any floating residue. Simmer gently for two hours, then strain through a fine sieve.

METHOD OF RISOTTO
Sweat the shallots and garlic in a little oil and butter in a pan at medium temperature for about 2 minutes, taking care that they do not colour. Add the rice, stir for 2 minutes more, then add the white wine. When absorbed, add a ladleful or two of hot quail stock. When the stock has been absorbed, add another ladleful, and continue to cook gently in this manner until the rice is almost cooked. At this point add the thyme leaves and the diced goats cheese. Complete the cooking of the risotto and keep warm.

METHOD OF QUAIL
Pre-heat the oven to 180°C/350°F/Gas Mark 4. Remove the legs (you can ask your butcher to do this for you) and retain for the stock. Season the quail with salt and pepper. Heat a little butter and oil in an ovenproof pan and seal the quail on all sides. Then roast for 7 minutes. Remove to a wire rack, rest for 6 minutes. Deglaze the pan with the quail stock and 10ml of the white wine, reduce and thicken with the remainder of the butter. Correct seasoning and set aside.

METHOD OF ORANGE CONFIT
Put everything except the oranges into a pan and bring to the boil. Simmer for an hour. Zest the oranges and add to the stock syrup. Leave to infuse for one hour, then drain and reserve the orange zest, and discard the syrup

TO COMPLETE AND SERVE
Cut the quail meat off the breast by running a knife gently down the breast bone and easing the flesh off the rib-cage. Shape some risotto using a ring cutter in the centre of each bowl, place the quail on top of the risotto, orange zest on top of the quail, and finally the pea shoots.

THE MANOR HOUSE
HOTEL AND GOLF CLUB

TO DRINK...

**Rioja Lan Gran
Reserva, Spain, 1996**
Opulent nose with red
fruit flavour, leather,
vanilla. Good tannin
and complex aromas
on the palate

ROSEMARY PANNA COTTA WITH CHERRY CRUMBLE (*serves 4-5*)

INGREDIENTS

PANNA COTTA
450ml double cream
50ml milk
2 sprigs fresh rosemary
75g caster sugar
1½ leaves gelatine

CHERRY COMPÔTE
500g fresh cherries
250ml water
250g sugar
Juice of half a lemon
1 tbs kirsch

FILO PASTRY CASE
3 sheets of filo pastry
50g maple syrup
25g butter

CRUMBLE TOPPING
100g butter (*cold*)
175g plain flour
40g caster sugar
40g demerara sugar
Pinch salt
1 tsp ground mixed spice

METHOD OF PANNA COTTA
Soak gelatine in a little cold water until soft. Put double cream, milk, sugar and rosemary sprigs into a saucepan and bring to the boil. Remove from the heat. Squeeze water from the gelatine, add to the hot mixture and mix thoroughly. When cold, strain into lightly oiled moulds. Refrigerate overnight.

METHOD OF CHERRY COMPÔTE
Stone the cherries, preferably using a cherry stoner. Bring the water, sugar, lemon juice and kirsch to the boil, add the cherries, cover with a lid and simmer for 15 minutes until tender. Blend half the cherries and 4 tablespoons of the syrup in a food processor or liquidiser. Drain the remaining cherries and mix with the purée.

METHOD OF CRUMBLE TOPPING
Preheat the oven to 150°C/300°F/Gas Mark 2. Sieve the flour, salt and ground mixed spice into a bowl. Add the butter cut into small cubes, and rub lightly through your fingers to make fine 'breadcrumbs'. Mix in the sugars, spread onto a baking tray and bake until golden brown. Break up with a fork while hot. Cool, then store in an airtight container.

METHOD OF FILO PASTRY CASE
Preheat the oven to 180°C/350°F/Gas Mark 4. Gently melt the maple syrup and butter together. Keeping the filo pastry covered with a damp cloth, brush the first filo pastry sheet with the maple syrup mix, brush two more sheets with the syrup mix and stack on top. Now cut large discs out of the stack, shape over lightly oiled metal moulds on a baking tray, and place another mould on top of each to hold it in place. Bake for 5 minutes. Remove the top mould and bake again until golden brown. Remove from the moulds while hot. When cold, store in an airtight container.

TO COMPLETE AND SERVE
Take the panna cotta from the fridge 30 minutes before serving. Gently heat the cherry compôte. Remove each panna cotta from its mould by holding it over the serving plate and gently pull away from one side. It should easily fall from the mould. Spoon cherry compôte into each filo pastry case, top with the crumble mix, and lightly dust the plate with icing sugar to prevent the crumble case from sliding around as you position it beside the panna cotta.

TO DRINK...

**Belgravia Late
Harvest, Australia,
2002**
Outrageously luscious,
pineapple glacé fruit,
botrytised orange
rind flavour

STRAWBERRY PAVLOVA (*serves* 10)

INGREDIENTS

PAVLOVA
5 large egg whites
(*should weigh 200g*)
Pinch salt
1/2 tsp vanilla essence
1 tbs white wine vinegar
280g caster sugar
25g cornflour

STRAWBERRY COULIS
900g fresh strawberries
300g icing sugar

STRAWBERRY FOOL
570ml double cream
200ml strawberry coulis
Juice of 1/2 lemon

Additional strawberries
and a sprig of mint to serve

METHOD OF PAVLOVA
Preheat the oven to 110°C/225°F/Gas Mark 1/4. Using an electric whisk, whisk together the egg whites, salt, vanilla essence, white wine vinegar and 140g of caster sugar until stiff peaks are formed. Mix together the remaining 140g caster sugar and the cornflour, and whisk this into the stiff egg whites. Do not overmix at this stage. Pipe onto trays lined with silicone mats (if possible) or baking paper, to form a round about 8cm in diameter and 6cm in depth. Place in the preheated oven for 1 hour until firm to the touch on the outside but still soft inside. Allow to cool, and store in an airtight container until required.

METHOD OF STRAWBERRY COULIS
Simply liquidize the hulled strawberries and the icing sugar to form a purée.

METHOD OF STRAWBERRY FOOL
Whisk all the ingredients together with an electric whisk until thick enough to hold a peak when the whisk is lifted out.

TO COMPLETE AND SERVE
Place the pavlova on a serving plate, using a little of the fool to hold it in place. Pipe the fool on top, creating a tall peak. Pour the coulis over the top so it runs down the sides in five or six places. Accompany with fresh strawberries cut up and bound with a little more of the coulis, and a sprig of fresh mint.

TO DRINK...

**Château du Seuil
Rosé 2004**
Light, dry with
a fruit finish

The Bybrook Restaurant

SCONES *(makes 12-15)*

INGREDIENTS

SCONES
500g self-raising flour
10g baking powder
$1/4$ tsp salt
125g butter
(*at room temperature*)
100g caster sugar
3 medium eggs
(*should weigh 125g*)
$1/2$ tsp vanilla essence
75g natural yoghurt
90ml milk
Extra milk for brushing

CHEF'S TIP

When cutting out the
scones, take care not to twist
the cutter. Just press down
and the sides should stay
straight during cooking.

METHOD
Preheat the oven to 150°C/300°F/Gas Mark 2. Sieve together the flour,
baking powder and salt. Place in a bowl with the sugar and butter and
rub lightly through your fingers until the mixture resembles fine
breadcrumbs. In another bowl, whisk together the eggs, yoghurt,
milk and vanilla essence. Add the liquid to the flour mixture and lightly
combine to form a soft dough. Cover with cling film and leave to rest
for 20 minutes. Turn out onto a lightly floured surface and knead gently
until smooth. Roll out until about 3cm thick. Keep the work surface well
floured to prevent the dough from sticking. Cut out the scones using
a 6cm round ring cutter. Turn upside-down and place on a baking tray
lined with baking paper. Brush the tops with milk. Place in the
preheated oven for 15-20 minutes until well risen and golden brown.

TO SERVE
Allow to cool slightly, split in half, and serve with clotted cream and
strawberry jam.

THE MANOR HOUSE
HOTEL AND GOLF CLUB

**Freshly-picked
mint tea, or Earl Grey**

the perfect picnic

SET IN 63 ACRES OF HAMPSHIRE PARKLAND WITH STUNNING VIEWS OF THE
SPECTACULAR AVENUE OF LIME TREES, LAINSTON IS THE IDEAL SPOT TO ENJOY
A PICNIC HAMPER ON THE LAWNS, AND IT'S AN ALL-YEAR-ROUND ACTIVITY.

Surrounded by some of the most beautiful countryside and exciting places to
visit in Hampshire, why not make things simpler by preparing a delicious picnic
hamper. When you find the perfect spot, spread out your picnic rug, unpack the
hamper and take in the breathtaking views as you delight in a sumptuous picnic.
We suggest a selection of finger sandwiches: smoked salmon, cucumber,
egg and Hampshire watercress, home-made scones with Dorset clotted cream
and preserve, chocolate éclairs, fruit cake, fruit tartlets and fresh local
strawberries. Accompany your afternoon tea with a bottle of champagne
- or something more traditional, such as Earl Grey or English Breakfast tea.

terrace food

BARBECUES ARE A TERRIFIC WAY TO ENTERTAIN IN A HUGE GROUP, BRINGING YOUR FAMILY AND FRIENDS TOGETHER AND PULLING OUT ALL THE STOPS IN THE GARDEN.

Pennyhill Park Hotel boasts a fantastic BBQ setting throughout the summer months in the terrace garden, and we have chosen to share with you some of the ideas of our highly experienced chefs to help you create perfect barbecued terrace dishes at home.

CHICKEN AND PRAWN KEBABS WITH LIME AND GINGER MARINADE *(serves 4)*

METHOD
Dice the chicken into 3cm pieces, removing any excess fat. Leave the prawns whole for that wow! factor. Cut the peppers in half, remove the seeds and cut into 3cm pieces. Slice the limes thickly. Divide the ingredients between the four skewers, alternating them as appropriate. Lay the prepared kebabs in a shallow container. Combine the marinade ingredients given, mix well, pour onto the kebabs and leave to marinate for at least an hour.

INGREDIENTS

KEBABS
600g chicken thigh meat
24 large peeled raw tiger prawns
(*no head, no tail, no shell*)
1 red pepper
1 green pepper
3 limes

MARINADE
250ml olive oil
3 limes, zested and juiced
75g root ginger, peeled and roughly chopped
75g honey
½ bunch coriander, roughly chopped
20g pink peppercorns, lightly crushed
Salt and pepper

You will need four metal skewers, 300mm long

CHEF'S TIP

Why not experiment with different fish, such as scallops, monkfish or salmon?

106

champagne and oysters

INGREDIENTS

12 rock oysters
2 shallots, finely diced
100ml red wine vinegar
1 lemon cut into
3 or more wedges

5 sprigs of dill and
crushed ice to serve

BUILT IN 1883 AS A FAMILY HOME, SOUTH LODGE STILL EXUDES THAT FEEL. AMONGST THE 93 ACRES OF PARKLAND ARE 260 VARIETIES OF RHODODENDRONS, CAMELLIAS AND AZALEAS. INSIDE THERE ARE 45 EXQUISITELY FURNISHED ROOMS, SOME WITH ROMANTIC FOUR-POSTER BEDS, BUBBLING JACUZZIS, AND WHICHEVER WAY YOU TURN THERE ARE STUNNING VIEWS OVER THE ROLLING SOUTH DOWNS.

Our luxurious granite-topped Champagne Bar is situated on our lower terrace and is the perfect place to enjoy a glass of bubbly with oysters as the sun sets.

OYSTERS (serves 4)

METHOD
Open the oysters with an oyster knife, cut loose from the shell and turn over, leave in the deeper part of the shell. Mix together the shallots and vinegar and pour into a shot glass.

TO SERVE
Place the crushed ice on a deep plate and place the shot glass in the middle. Arrange the 12 oysters around the plate on the ice, with a lemon wedge or two between every third oyster. Place the dill sprigs around the base of the shot glass and serve immediately.

buggy food

AFTER A LONG DAY'S GOLF, WHAT COULD BE MORE REWARDING THEN A HEARTY TRADITIONAL ENGLISH MEAL! WHETHER YOU HAVE ENJOYED A ROUND WITH US AT MANNINGS HEATH, OR ARE RETURNING HOME FROM A LEISURELY ROUND AT YOUR LOCAL COURSE, IMAGINE TUCKING INTO A LARGE PLATE OF BANGERS 'N' MASH - THE SUCCULENT TASTE OF SIZZLING QUALITY SAUSAGES IN FRESHLY MADE CREAMY MASH SOAKED IN ONION GRAVY. WHAT COULD TASTE BETTER?

SAUSAGE AND MASHED POTATO (serves 4)

INGREDIENTS

12 sausages

MASHED POTATO
4 large potatoes
200ml cream
Salt and pepper

CABBAGE BALLS, CARROTS, CARAMELISED ONIONS
1 Savoy cabbage
4 carrots
4 white onions
250g unsalted butter
Salt and pepper

SAUCE
4 onions, finely chopped
Butter
1 pint of beef gravy
250ml red wine
Salt and pepper

CHEF'S TIP

Make sure you pat the cabbage leaves dry so there will be less moisture and more flavour in the cabbage balls.

Take your time with the caramelised onions, as rushing with a high heat can result in a bitter taste.

METHOD OF CABBAGE BALLS
Peel four large outer leaves from the cabbage, wash and pat dry. Remove stalk and slice the remainder. Peel and dice one onion and soften in a frying pan with a little oil. Add the cabbage and cook together until soft. Check seasoning. Cut two large squares of cling film and overlap them. Place one large cabbage leaf in the centre with some of the cabbage mixture on top. Bring all four corners of the cling film in to the middle to form a ball. Repeat the process with the other leaves.

METHOD OF MASHED POTATO
Wash, peel and quarter the potatoes. Place in cold water, bring to the boil and simmer until soft. Drain. Add cream, season and mash until smooth.

METHOD OF SAUSAGES
Place under a hot grill and cook turning occasionally until golden brown all over. (Do not prick the sausages as this will release the flavour.)

METHOD OF SAUCE
Fry the onions in butter until soft and golden. Add the red wine followed by the beef gravy and gently boil. Check seasoning to taste.

METHOD OF CARROTS
Wash, peel, and trim the carrots. Cut them into small cylinders, put into cold salted water, bring to the boil and simmer until just cooked.

METHOD OF CARAMELISED ONIONS
Peel and slice the remaining onions. Melt the butter in a pan over a gentle heat, add the onions and cook until caramelised. This will take about 30-35 minutes.

TO SERVE
Pipe a base of mashed potato onto the plate, pour a pool of sauce over it, and place three sausages on top. Reheat the cabbage ball and place next to the Bangers 'n' Mash, then arrange the carrots and a rounded spoonful of caramelised onions alongside. Serve extra sauce separately.

room service

THE PERFECT END TO A PERFECT DAY IS BEING TUCKED UP NICE AND WARM WITH YOUR HOME COMFORTS SURROUNDING YOU. AT THE MANOR HOUSE THIS IS SOMETHING WE PRIDE OURSELVES ON, WITH OUR COTSWOLD STONE COTTAGES, WHICH ARE ALL DESIGNED AS ENCHANTING ROOMS AND HAVE A CHARM OF THEIR OWN.

This is the perfect place to simply curl up in front of a log fire with a large glass of wine and a dish to warm you through and through. Recreate this vision at home by putting together this mushroom risotto, pour yourself a glass of mellow wine, cosy up to your fire and really savour the whole experience.

RISOTTO WITH WILD MUSHROOMS (serves 4-6)

INGREDIENTS

1 litre chicken stock
50g butter
2 shallots, finely chopped
1 tsp chopped garlic
300g Arborio rice
300g selection of wild mushrooms, cleaned/washed and trimmed
100ml white wine
50g parmesan cheese, finely grated
25g chopped parsley
Sea salt
Ground pepper
2 bunches asparagus

METHOD
Heat the chicken stock. Melt half the butter in a large saucepan, add the shallots, then the garlic, and cook gently for a few minutes. Add the rice and stir for another minute, coating the rice in butter. Pour in the wine and allow to bubble, then stir and start adding the hot chicken stock, a little at a time. As the rice absorbs the stock, keep adding more little by little, while stirring to ensure the rice cooks evenly and to prevent it from sticking. Meanwhile, in another saucepan melt the remaining butter and gently fry the mushrooms until cooked; season with salt and pepper. Trim the asparagus tips to about 7cm, and cook for a few minutes in boiling salted water.

TO SERVE
When the rice is tender, combine with the mushrooms, chopped parsley and parmesan. Garnish with the asparagus tips and serve immediately.

organic food

IN A WORLD EVER MORE HEALTH CONSCIOUS, ORGANIC FOOD IS BECOMING MORE AND MORE POPULAR. PEOPLE ARE TURNING TO THEIR SUPERMARKETS FOR FOOD THAT IS HOME GROWN AND TASTES NATURAL. THE SPA AT PENNYHILL PARK IS AN ORGANIC SPA AND A HAVEN OF RELAXATION; OUR CAFÉ THEMIS WORKS WITH ORGANIC PRODUCE TO CREATE FABULOUS FOOD AND DRINK.

With organic produce becoming more easily available, and with healthy eating being an important part of most people's everyday life and a major part of The Spa's ethos, we decided to produce a recipe using organic foods. Something easy to create, that tastes exceptional and is good for you.

CHILLED CUCUMBER SOUP WITH SEARED SMOKED SALMON (serves 4)

METHOD
Blend all the soup ingredients together. Pass through a fine sieve into a bowl. Season and adjust the consistency as required. If too thin, add more yoghurt; if too thick, mix together some yoghurt and water and stir in. Refrigerate. Prepare all the ingredients for the potato salad. Mix them together and firmly pack into suitable moulds, such as stainless steel rings 7cm wide. Allow to set in the fridge. Wash the salad leaves and choose small pieces of each variety to garnish the top of each smoked salmon steak. Combine the leaves together gently, cover and place in the fridge till needed.

TO SERVE
Sear the smoked salmon steaks on both sides for an attractive colour, using a griddle pan if you have one. Serve the smoked salmon and the quail eggs at room temperature. Place a potato salad ring in the centre of each bowl, leaving the ring in place. Pour the soup carefully into the bowl, to come about three-quarters of the way up the potato salad, then remove the ring. Place the salmon on top of the potato, garnish with your prepared leaves and place a halved quail egg in the centre of each one. Put some of the larger salad leaves in a small bowl, dress with olive oil and serve alongside.

INGREDIENTS

4 x 115g steaks cut from a side of unsliced smoked salmon, with no skin
4 quail eggs, boiled for 1-2 minutes, chilled in cold water, then peeled

CUCUMBER SOUP
2 cucumbers, peeled and deseeded
1kg Greek yoghurt
$^{1}/_{2}$ bunch mint leaves

POTATO SALAD
300g boiled potatoes, peeled and cut into 1cm dice
$^{1}/_{2}$ bunch chopped chives
50g chopped shallots
4 limes, zested
75g mayonnaise
Smoked salmon trimmings

SALAD LEAVES
Lollo rosso, frisée, wild rocket, chervil

Olive oil
Maldon salt and pepper

CHEF'S TIP

Ask your local fishmonger or supermarket if they can cut the smoked salmon for you. You may find that you need to order it ahead of time.

Acknowledgements

EXCLUSIVE HOTELS WOULD LIKE TO THANK THE FOLLOWING SUPPLIERS FOR THEIR SUPPORT IN PRODUCING THE 'EXCLUSIVE TASTES' COOKBOOK.

Allied Domecq
Prewetts Mill
Worthing Road
Horsham RH12 1ST
01403 222600

Arthur Rackham Emporia Wine Merchants
216 London Road
Burpham, Guildford
Surrey GU4 7JS
01483 458700

Bonnet UK Ltd
3 Crusader Industrial Estate
Stirling Road
Cressex Business
High Wycombe HP12 3XX
01494 464470

Coopers Seafood
Unit H
The Alexander Bell Centre
Andover SP10 3UR
01264 337299

Fairfax Meadow
24 27 Regis Road
Kentish Town
London NW5 3EZ

Haines Farm Eggs
Clappers Farm Lane
Mortimer
Reading RG7 2LG
0118 933 3344

Hatto & Son
116 Frimley Road
Camberley GU15 2QN
01276 65757

Horsham Laundry
Unit D, Foundy Close
Horsham RH13 5TX
01403 263108

S K Hutchings Butchers
Myers House
High Street
Partridge Green RH13 8HU
01403 710209

Premier Cheese
124 Gregories Road
Beaconsfield HP9 1HT

Premier Fish Ltd
Unit 2, Scotts Close
Batten Road
Downtown
Salisbury SP5 3RA
01725 513398

Pro Chef Catering Equipment
Unit 9-10, Belton Road
Industrial Estate
Grantham NG31 9HN
01476 569652

Pure Oyster Co Ltd
Imperial House
Old Brighton Road
Pease Pottage RH11 9NG
01293 549843

Rational UK Ltd
Unit 4 Titan Court
Laporte Way
Porten Way Business Park
Luton LU4 8EF
01582 480388

Reynolds Catering Supplies Ltd
Balch House
New Spitalfields Market
25 Sherrin Road
Leyton
London E10 5SQ
0845 310 6200

Scottish Courage Ltd
PO Box 1938
Livingston
Edinburgh EH54 8YF
0845 302 3000

Springs Smoked Salmon
Edburton
Henfield BH5 9LN
01273 857338

Upstream Seafood Ltd
6 Horatius Way
Croydon CR0 4RU
02086 671251

WickWar Brewing Co
Station Road
Wickwar
Gloucester GL12 8NB
01454 294168

WITH GRATEFUL THANKS ALSO TO CREATIVE AND BRAND LTD FOR DESIGNING AND PUBLISHING THE BOOK, TO MARTIN BRENT FOR THE FANTASTIC PHOTOGRAPHY, TO JANE ROWELL FOR PROOFREADING AND EDITING, TO DEBBIE GUY AS THE MENTOR FOR THE MDP TEAM COOKBOOK AND TO EVERYONE WHO SUPPORTED THIS PROJECT FROM DAY ONE TO FINAL PRODUCTION.

The Cookbook Story

The Management Development Programme (MDP) is developed by Exclusive Hotels. It consists of a year's course with six Management modules, designed to teach future managers the skills they need to succeed within the business.

Each year a group of students are selected from across all the Exclusive properties. We are six of the 2004/2005 students: Alison Warren from The Spa, Clare Howland from Pennyhill Park, Sarah Rowden from Lainston House, Peter Williams from South Lodge, Massimo Perna from The Manor House and Angela Todd from Mannings Heath Golf Club.

Halfway through the year we are placed into three project groups, and given a business-based project to complete and present on our final day. This gives us an opportunity to demonstrate our business acumen, showing how we have investigated, developed and implemented a business plan to produce the completed project. We were group C-Product. We were to produce, design, market and launch an Exclusive Hotels Cookbook.

Throughout this project, the six of us have all learnt so much. From budgeting, researching, learning about book layout and design, photographing food, deciding on the name, working with the chefs, to marketing the final product to become something exceptional. We have worked very hard to produce our cookbook, combining everything that we have learnt on the MDP into every issue we have had to face on a daily basis.

September 5th, 2005 was the day of our final presentations: 3 groups all desperate to win, all pulling out the stops, the standards extremely high. The champagne flowed on the news that Team Cookbook had won the 'Group of the Year' award. Words can't describe our feelings that night, and we were all so proud of each other.

When we began the MDP we never thought we would finish it having produced this amazing Cookbook. We continue to feel proud to have been a part of this huge investment, and thank Danny Pecorelli for this amazing chance.

We hope you have been amazed by 'Exclusive Tastes' and that it has inspired you to get as passionate about food as we have.

Alison, Claire, Sarah, Peter, Massimo and Angela
TEAM COOKBOOK